William Ramsey

Spiritualism

a satanic delusion and a sign of the times

William Ramsey

Spiritualism
a satanic delusion and a sign of the times

ISBN/EAN: 9783337301965

Printed in Europe, USA, Canada, Australia, Japan

Cover: Foto ©Lupo / pixelio.de

More available books at **www.hansebooks.com**

SPIRITUALISM,

A

SATANIC DELUSION,

AND

A SIGN OF THE TIMES.

BY WILLIAM RAMSEY, D.D.,

PASTOR OF THE CEDAR STREET PRESBYTERIAN CHURCH, PHILADELPHIA.

EDITED WITH A PREFACE,

BY H. L. HASTINGS.

"The God of peace shall bruise Satan under your feet shortly."—Rom. xvi: 20.

PEACE DALE, R. I.:
PUBLISHED BY H. L. HASTINGS.
1856.

EDITOR'S PREFACE.

The subject of spiritual agencies, and the investigation of their mysterious operations, is one of deep interest to mankind. From the earliest ages it has afforded ground for superstition, investigation, and speculation. Various as the theories of the present are found to be, they all, or nearly all, have their counterparts in the dim distance of ages past, and within the period covered by historic records, both sacred and profane.

The belief in a race of invisible and superhuman agents, who are, more or less intimately concerned in terrestrial affairs, is found in all past ages, and is common alike to the Jews and the Barbarians, to the wise and the unwise, to Christians and to heathen.

The subject has always been interesting. It is now increasing in interest, from the fact that attention has been called to it, and investigations have been made to a much greater extent than heretofore, especially since "Spiritualism" has become the faith of millions, and the amazement of millions more.—The writer had hoped ere this to have presented to the public a statement of the results of his researches on the subject; he still hopes to do so in due time, if God permit. The subject is ample; the field wide.

The present treatise by a learned and able student and theologian, who was for years a missionary to India, and was there conversant with the various oriental forms of supernatural influences, will be found interesting; and, brief as it is, the writer has seen nothing that meets the requirements of the case so fully as this little treatise.

The Bible is made the basis of the argument. Some Spiritualists will object to this. To such, we will say that the *foundations* upon which *that* rests are neither *known* nor *assailed* as yet, by most who reject it with puny contempt. When they have given years to such investigations as those of Lardener, Keith, Paley, and others; when they have answered and refuted the arguments of such men as Leslie and Lyttleton, and countless writers who have studied the subject; *then* they may have some claim to speak with a degree of assurance. But modesty is the truest wisdom of those who, in cavilling at Christianity, "speak evil of things that they know not of," and whose very cavils are proofs that they know neither the doctrines of the Bible, nor the facts upon which its authority rests.

Upon a basis—not of sacerdotal authority, but of sound reason; not of mere theory, but of stubborn *facts*—we rest the foundations of our faith. We do not take the truths of the Bible for *granted*, we take them as *proved*, and proved by a mass of evidence which has accumulated for ages, and which infidels and sceptics have never met, or tried to meet. With this basis, we proceed to test the veracity and reliability of those spirits who come to us from their various spheres, and who seek to win our assent to the propositions which they promulgate.

In characterizing Spiritualism as " A Satanic Delusion," we would speak not in contempt, but in words of solemn and earnest admonition. We would speak as those who must give an account, and would most affectionately strive to teach those who desire information, the perils that beset their course. In hope that this treatise may commend itself to the candor of an enlightened public, it is now committed to them. That it contains much truth, we doubt not; that it will subvert or destroy the rapidly increasing influence of Spiritualism, we do not expect. But if it shall prevent *some* from risking their eternal well-being in a most perilous path; if it shall strengthen the faith of any who are perplexed with doubts and waverings; if it shall be a means of recovering any from the snare of the fowler ere it be too late; if it shall glorify God, exalt and honor His truth, and lead any to prepare and wait for the day of the Church's redemption, when God shall bruise Satan under their feet, then the labor will not have been in vain in the Lord.

That it may accomplish some good, and, in the workings of Divine Providence, bring forth some fruit to the good of man and the glory of God, is alike the prayer of the author and the editor.   H. L. H.

PEACE DALE, R. I., *June*, 1856.

SPIRITUALISM

A

SATANIC DELUSION.

CHAPTER I.

Introduction.

The object of the present investigation is, to ascertain the character of modern Spiritualism and its significance as a sign of the Times.

This subject is one that presents to the mind of the thoughtful reader of the Word of God, and the careful observer of the workings of Satan in these last days, such a wide field for remark, that we scarcely know where to begin, what facts to select, or where to end. It is certain that we are now living in strange and eventful times. There are agencies at work in our world other than can be seen by the eye of man. But this has always been the case.— The facts in reference to the fall of man, and his redemption by Christ, show us most clearly, that there are opposing agencies at work in reference to his present and future state that are outside of himself; and that man is that most important being who concentrates the thoughts of the whole invisible world upon him.

The educational training of some, and the manifest ignorance of others of the truths of the Bible, the only true revelation of the will of God to man, hinder multitudes from admitting, in all their literality and distinctness, the statements of the Word of God on the subject of Spirit-agency. In consequence of this, reasonings on this subject, the most false, puerile, and stupid, often pass at par for sound logic and good scriptural argument, provided they be clothed in the garb of scientific words and technical phraseology, the true meaning of which the people cannot comprehend, and one grand design of which is, in reality, to conceal the ignorance of the men themselves, who attempt to explain what they do not understand, and who are, though unconscious to themselves, another illustration of the wonderful power of that influence, the very existence of which they so stoutly deny.

There are many good men in our midst, highly gifted, and deservedly esteemed for their scientific researches and their patient investigation of the causes of things, who are bold to say that the phenomena of Modern Spiritualism, are mere optical illusions, or juggling tricks, and that all of them can easily be explained upon scientific principles, and are well understood by those who perform them. Yea, more; boasting of their fancied wisdom and knowledge of things beyond their reach, they are not slow to say that to believe in the facts as they exist is a sad proof of a defective education, if not of imbecility of mind. But these persons, with more correctness, might say that the solutions which they and their philosophic expounders give of these latter day wonders, ascribing them all to mere natural agents, as electricity, magnetism, odic force, and we know not what else, are still more striking illustrations of the very deficiency which they so feelingly lament in the case of others.

At all events, one thing is certain : those who hold that there is a spiritual agency in connection with these manifestations, have a cause which is adequate to the production of these effects—yea, and, if need be, of others far more wonderful than any that have as yet been exhibited. They go to the Word of God for a clear and proper solution of all these phenomena, and not to the mysterious workings of some hidden law of nature, nor to the teachings of an Infidel or Atheistic Philosophy.

The writers of the Sacred Scriptures nowhere attempt to prove the existence of God. Moses takes it for granted, and proceeds to state, in the first chapters of Genesis, what God has created. Nor do they attempt to prove the existence of a Spiritual Being, whom they call in the Hebrew, Satan; which means an opposer, a foe, an enemy. They speak of it as a fact that needs no proof; for the world is full of the evidences of his real, personal existence, and of his mighty power, and unremitted hatred of God and of man. We are fully aware of the fact that the personal existence of Satan is admitted by nearly all those who bear the Christian name. It is at least among the articles of their faith. But by the great majority of professing Christians of the present day, it is so feebly realized, and so superficially regarded, that their faith is, in a great degree, inoperative, and the fact of his existence, and influence upon the minds of the people, is virtually disbelieved. One striking difference between the experience of Christians, as recorded in the New Testament, and the frequent exhortations of our Lord and his apostles to resist the Devil, and to guard against his wiles, and the experience of Christians of our day, and the exhortations we hear on the subject now, warning us not to be ignorant of his devices, must be manifest to every one who will give the subject a moment's reflection. They felt and acted as if there was a great and mighty adversary for them to oppose; and they speak of their spiritual conflicts with him; but the wisdom and philosophy of our day have looked upon his existence as a myth, or at best, but another name for the wayward disposition of man.

This, however, is not the scriptural representation of the matter. The Bible speaks of him as a mighty spirit, once holy, but now fallen through pride; as the deceiver of man; as the usurper of the dominion of this world, and as the Prince of this world, and also of the power of the air, and the Spirit that worketh in the children of disobedience.— Through his influence and wiles, our first parents lost the image and the likeness of God in which they were created, and also the dominion over the earth which God had bestowed on man. Satan deposed man, and took his place. Since then he has not ceased to exert his influence over man; to enslave his mind by gross superstitions; to debase and defile his body by vile affections; to shut him out of heaven by leaguing him in with himself in opposition to God. Accordingly we find that although the agent, Satan, is the same at all times, yet the mode of his operations differs in different ages and among different people, according to the degree of their intellectual culture, or the amount of Scriptural truth and knowledge they might possess.

The debasing and sensual rights of Paganism are well adapted to rivet the chains of a spiritual bondage upon a people who have given up the knowledge of a true God, and who worship demons in His stead. But in an age like ours, where intellectualism and mammon are the gods to which the masses of the people bow in humble adoration, Satan must suit his wiles to the spirit of the age, and to the character of the people, if he would succeed in leading them to bow down to their gods, in the temple of reason, and to ignore their Creator and the revelation he has given them. Hence it is that no special form of Satanic delusion continues long at one time, or in one place. The Arch-Deceiver continually varies his wiles. Old forms of spiritual delusion pass away; but from their seeds other forms spring up, which are just as far from the truth as the former.—Each successive age or generation boasts of its freedom from the follies of the past, and laughs at the ignorance and superstition of their fathers, while it is itself the victim of those Satanic delusions which are more in accordance with the circumstances, advanced knowledge, or philosophic spirit of the age. And just as we change our garments and adapt them to the season of the year upon which we may enter, while our nature remains the same—so will it be with these varied exhibitions of Satanic power; their forms differ, but their essential features are the same; and these varied manifestations will continue to come and to go, until the kingdom of Satan, on earth, be overthrown, the reign of sin be superseded by that of holiness, and the kingdoms of this world become the kingdom of our Lord and of His Christ.

As the sacred writers nowhere attempt to prove the personal existence of Satan, but always take it for granted, (and base their exhortations to resist his power and influence, upon the known fact of his existence and evil character,) we need not attempt it. Still, we might ask those who deny the personal existence of Satan, and maintain that we are to understand by the term only the evil principle, or the tendency to evil that exists in human nature, how they would explain, on their theory, the history of the fall of man, and the subsequent temptation of our Lord? In the case of Adam, or rather of the woman, (for she was first in the transgression, she being deceived, while "Adam was not deceived"—1. Tim. ii: 14—but sinned understandingly,) there was evidently an influence outside of herself that was brought to bear upon her mind, so that she yielded to it and fell—she was conscious of that fact—and said so: nor is the truth of her statement called in question by the Lord when she, in the honesty of her heart, confessed the truth, saying, "the serpent beguiled me, and I did eat." The statement was admitted, in all its fullness, and upon that statement the Lord proceeds, at once, to pronounce His sentence upon the serpent, and which remains upon it, to the present day, and will till time shall end. The Judge of all the earth certainly does right. And if there were no tempter outside of woman, why should the Lord pronounce His curse upon her, and an additional one on a being, distinct from her, if no such being did exist, and if he had not deceived her as she declared he did?

So also, in the case of our Lord. He had no sin. He was holy, harmless, undefiled, and separate from sinners. And yet He was tempted for forty days and forty nights in the wilderness of Judea. Demands were made of Him and proposals offered of such a character, as wholly to exclude the idea, (if we admit the record in the case to be true,) of these demands and proposals being the mere suggestions of our Lord's own mind. The thing is an impossibility. To suppose that the whole scene of the temptation as described by the inspired penman was a mere stretch of the imagination of our Lord; that He thought He was tempted by some one; that He thought the Tempter brought forth arguments based upon a false application of the Scriptures to induce Him to yield to his suggestions; and, that He thought He answered the Tempter by correct quotations from the Word of God, requires an amount of faith (if faith it may be called,) far surpassing any thing of the kind that is necessary to embrace the simple, truthful narration of the facts as they are. But it happens to be with such persons as it was with a Brahmin in India, who said to me once, "Sahib, a little truth is hard, but a big lie is easy to be believed." It is just so; and we doubt not, that the father of lies assists them in their monstrous credulity as well as in their unreasonable unbelief.

We admit the fact, then, in all its fullness, that there is such a being as Satan, and we fully believe all the statements that the Sacred Scriptures give of him, and of his workings in our world. Our Lord calls him "the Prince of this world," and the "god of this world;" and he is. That he will, ere long, be deposed, and his usurped power will be taken from him, and he be cast out of this world, are facts clearly made known to us in the Word of God. He knows well that the kingdoms of this world will be taken from him, and that it will be done by Him who is "the seed of the woman." Hence it was that Satan offered to deliver up to our Lord the kingdoms of the world, which he then held, and still holds by usurpation, if He, the Messiah, would but fall down and do him honor, or thank him for them, or even accept them from his hand. We give Satan full credit for honesty in this case. Let him have his due. We believe he would have done just as he said he would do. He had the kingdoms of the world. He has them yet.* And he, doubtless, would have deliv-

---

* For Satan to offer that which he could not bestow, and over

ered them to our Lord, and would have laid down the usurped sceptre of power over earth, if he could, by that act, have acquired a greater glory, and a more exalted sway. And who, in the matters of trade, and of seeking after the wealth and the honors of this world, would not part with the less for the sake of the greater? So with Satan. The honor received from man, or from a world of men, would be as naught when compared with honor and obeisance from " the Son of man." Most cheerfully would he have parted with all this world for one act of obeisance from our Lord. But, that he must not have. Satan was foiled in his deep-laid scheme for the final and eternal ruin of all the human race. No compromise in the case can be made with the Son of man, the rightful heir to earth, and all upon it. Satan will not resign his usurped authority and power on earth of his own free will, nor can the Son of man lay aside the glory and the dignity of His exalted nature and office, to enter upon any efforts of negociation with Satan for the redemption of the world from his power. On the contrary, He will in due time, lay hold on the usurper, bind him in chains, and cast him out of the governments of this world for ever.

Satan is fully aware of this fact. He knew when our Lord was upon the earth, that that was not the time for

which he had no power, would be no temptation even to *man*, much less to *Christ*, who of course knew the *facts* in the case.— But Christ *was* really *tempted*—therefore Satan had something of value to offer to him, namely, the kingdoms of the world and their glory. Christ was tempted in all points like as we are, and do we not see in the allurements of worldly ambition that seduce the heart from *right* and *godliness*, this same temptation of the adversary ? We are not ignorant of his devices.—ED.

his dethronement. But the time is now at hand. This he knows; and hence it is that he is making special efforts, in various ways, throughout the whole world, to retain his possession of the earth to the last moment, and to ruin for time and eternity all he can, before he himself shall be cast out, and be shut up in the bottomless pit for the thousand years.

Paganism and the gross forms of heathen idolatry, are not adapted to our present enlightened and social state.—The scenes of iniquity that have been witnessed in the public assembly, or in the secret chambers of heathen temples, in days past, would be too much at present for the eye of the refined of our day. But similar scenes may be witnessed, doubtless, even now, by those who are privileged to enter within the gates that shut them out from the vulgar gaze. It only needs another name: the name of "Love," or " Love" made " free," and the sanction of laws which Satan himself has helped to frame, to give currency and popularity to any forms of iniquity that have ever yet found favor in the eyes of a world at enmity with God. Some can be led as the willing slaves of their lusts. For these there is a lure in the shape of Socialism, Free-love-ism, and Mormonism, that last form of political iniquity that has been enthroned in our land, and which if it receives not the sanction of this mighty nation, is permitted to grow unmolested, and to flourish in our midst, under the fostering care of Satan himself.

But, there are others, whose instinctive horror of bodily defilement would separate them forever from those, who " corrupt themselves in those things which, as brute beasts, they know naturally" (Jude 10). These Satan must secure by other means. Reason is their god. To them, the revelations of the Most High are, at least, but enigmatical hints of things they cannot comprehend. For the god of this world hath blinded their minds, lest the light of the glorious gospel of Christ, who is the image of God, should shine into their hearts, and give them the light of the knowledge of the glory of God in the face of Jesus Christ, 2 Cor. iv. 4-6. They must have certain knowledge, and such a knowledge of secret and future things, as God, in His infinite wisdom, withholds from man; for he would have man "walk by faith, not by sight," 2 Cor. v. 7. But, what God withholds, Satan offers to impart. They would lift the veil that hides the unseen world from them, and seek to know from those who inhabit it, the things which God has hidden from them, and purposes they shall not know. The knowledge of Satan is not like ours. We can know nothing of the invisible world from our own observation. Satan can and does.— The invisible world is all untrodden ground to us. To him it is all known and familiar. He, doubtless, does and can know facts, and reveal them too, which it would gratify the curiosity of our nature to know. Facts, long since transpired, even before the birth of any now on earth, are not blotted out of the memory of Satan, who, we may suppose, retains all the knowledge he has ever had of our world for the past 6000 years. These facts he may communicate to man, (and none can prove that he cannot); and these facts being found to be true, the door is now opened wide for the full belief of any number, or any kind of real or supposed facts that Satan may see fit to communicate. The reality of one truth will pave the way for many falsehoods, all of which may be believed with equal faith. In this way, Satan will satisfy the minds of multitudes of the philosophically wise. And as they judge they can find that knowledge in and through his communications which they cannot obtain from the Word of God, the result is easily foreseen. They will reject the revelation which God has given them, as a work behind the age, and not meeting the demands of the times. If this be not so with those who now believe in the revelations that God has made to them in His Word, they will superadd to it these supposed revelations of facts by Satan, and thus will they virtually set aside the Word of God entirely as a rule of life.

As it is certainly revealed to us, that Satan will be cast out from this world, and as his efforts will be made untiringly to retain his hold upon the minds of the people, we may reasonably look for some special manifestations of his power and delusive workings before that event. These manifestations and miraculous workings will be so apparent to all those, who are savingly enlightened by the Spirit of God, that they will not fail to perceive, in due time, that they are of Satanic origin. "They that trust in the Lord shall be," in these times of coming trial, "as Mount Zion which cannot be removed, but abideth forever," Ps. cxxv. 1. While those who may trust to their own fallible reasoning and the desires of their hearts, will be as the chaff before the wind, or as the stubble before the flame.

By multitudes of Christians in our day, and of Christian ministers also, the study of the prophecies of God's Word is either neglected, or condemned. What God declares to be "a light that shineth in a dark place, until the day dawn and the Day-Star arise" (2 Peter i. 19), they, in their presumption have declared to be impenetrable obscurity.—Hence the utter misapprehension which so extensively prevails in the Church at the present time, as to the character and design and end of this dispensation. Peace, prosperity and stability are confidently predicted and fondly anticipated by the men of our progressive times; whereas conflict and destruction are distinctly foretold by the prophets of the Lord. And so intense is this deception, that, by many, the very workings of Satan are confounded with or taken for the operations of God's Spirit. They look for a coming glory and a brighter age for this world; but it is not such as God predicts. They raise their superstructure, Babel-like, out of material which God purposes to destroy. There is a future glory in reserve for this world. But, it is not to be effected by the wisdom of man, the progressive development of the age, nor by a careful observance and study of the mere laws of nature. It will be the work of the Spirit and power of the Lord.

CHAPTER II.

THE CASE STATED.

That we may the better understand the nature of these spiritual manifestations, which now exist in our world, and which will continue to increase, though they will, doubtless, be varied in their form, until Satan himself, the grand originator of them all, shall be cast out of this world, it may be well to take a brief survey of his operations, in our world, from the fall of man to the present time. " To the law and to the testimony," the revealed will of God, let us then go for the true light that we need on this subject. If we speak not according to this word, it is because there is no light in us.—Is. viii : 20. The opinions of Pagan, of Jewish, and of Christian writers on this subject, are not without their value. But our object is to look at this whole subject in the light which the inspired Word of God throws upon it.

Taking then, in our hand, the inspired volume, the Word of God, "as a lamp to our path, and a light to our feet," let us enter the garden of Eden. There we find nature smiling in her garments of glory, as she was first robed by the hand of her all-wise and bountiful Creator.

Creatures, formed by the Divine Word, and exhibiting at the same time, the wisdom, the goodness, and the power of God, dwelt in peace and harmony with each other. There was no ferocity in any nature. There was no enmity in any heart. Man, created in the image of God, and according to His likeness, with his beloved and sinless companion by his side, the progenitor of the race of man on the earth, stood up in all the Godlike dignity of his nature, the installed king over earth and all the creatures that dwelt upon it. How long this primeval state of purity, of blessedness and of peace remained, we know not. On this point the Word of God sheds no light. We simply know the fact that man was sinless, and that he fell.

Before the creation of man, a rebellion against the authority of God, broke out among the angels in the heavenly world. Satan led the way. Insolence, pride, ambition, a being puffed up (as the Greek word *tuphotheis*, 1 Tim. ii. 16, signifies), in consequence, probably, of some exalted honor conferred upon him by his Creator, led to his sin. Multitudes must have united with him in his schemes and plans of rebellion against God, whatever they may have been.— But in their plans they failed. They lost the glory that they formerly possessed, and henceforth they were deprived of the favor of God, and were shut out from all communion with God, and with the holy angels. On the particular sin of Satan, and the precise time when he first transgressed, the Bible reveals nothing positive, and hence we cannot know with certainty, what it was, or when it took place.— The only thing we do know, is that it was before the fall of man, and that Satan was instrumental in that fall. This must satisfy us now.

There is a great and important fact here, which it may be well to consider a moment. . It is one of those mysteries which we cannot now fully comprehend, but we may hereafter. The fact is this: Although Satan and his angels are shut out from all communion and fellowship with God and the holy angels, still, they are not wholly debarred from all communication with heaven and holy beings. The testimony of the Bible is clear on this point, though Christians may seldom think of it, or if they do, may reject it without much thought. Twice in the book of Job, viz: chap. i. 6, and ii. 1, we are told that there was a day when the sons of God, the holy angels, came to present themselves before the Lord, and Satan came also among them to present himself before the Lord. While there, the Lord spoke to him and asked him, "From whence comest thou?" To which Satan replied, "From going to and fro in the earth, and walking up and down in it." Or, as the Septuagint renders it—"Having gone round the earth, and having walked over all that is under heaven, I am come hither."

In 1 Kings xxii. 19, Micah, the prophet, saw the Lord sitting upon his throne, and all the host of heaven standing before Him, on His right hand and on His left. "And the Lord said, who shall persuade Ahab that he may go up and fall at Ramoth-Gilead? And one said on this manner, and another said on that manner. And there came forth a spirit, and stood before the Lord, and said, I will persuade him. And the Lord said unto him, wherewith? And he said, I will go forth and will be a lying spirit in the mouth of all his prophets. And He said, thou shalt persuade him, and prevail also; go forth and do so." We would merely remark here, that God in scriptural language, is often said to do what he permits to be done.

Again, Zechariah, the prophet, chap. iii. 1, "saw Joshua, the High Priest, standing before the angel of the Lord, and Satan standing at His right hand to resist him. And the Lord said to Satan, the Lord rebuke thee, O, Satan."

In Jude, verse 9, we read that "Michael, the Archangel,

when contending with the devil, he disputed about the body of Moses, durst not bring against him a railing accusation, (or, as the Greek might be read, did not pass judgment upon him for blasphemy, but referred the case to the Lord,) saying, the Lord rebuke thee."

Again, in Rev. xii, the same thing is brought to our view. There we are told that there is to be a war in heaven—Michael and his angels fighting against Satan and his angels. And the Dragon and his angels were cast out of heaven.—Their place was found no more in heaven. Satan, who deceived the whole world, was cast out into the earth, and his angels were cast out with him. Then it is, after Satan's complete expulsion from all access to the heavenly beings, and from his long held empire in the air, that we hear the heavenly hosts, who never sinned against God, and the ransomed Church from earth, proclaiming with a loud voice in heaven, "now is come salvation and strength, and the kingdom of our God and the power of His Christ; for the Accuser of our brethren is cast down, who accused them before God day and night. Then there is rejoicing in heaven by the angels, and the ransomed Church; but there is woe to the inhabiters of the earth and of the sea, for the Devil is come down to the earth, having great wrath, for he hath but a short time then to remain upon it.

Now, without attempting to enter into any critical examination, or extended explanation of these passages already quoted, we learn from them several important facts, some of which we will here state. We learn,

1. That Satan, and it may be evil spirits, are not wholly debarred from all communication with God, and the holy angels. It does not appear that they have any intercourse

with them further than their coming in conflict with them and opposing them.

2. That God still uses these evil spirits, as the instruments in His hands of punishing those who may reject his counsels, and that when they are permitted to afflict the good, it is never done unless God intends to bring out of the affliction a greater good to the afflicted, and glory to His own great name.

3. That these evil spirits may take possession of men in the flesh, and control them as the lying spirit took possession of the Prophets of Ahab, and thus deceived him, if God permit them to do so.

4. That the power of these evil spirits will be more wonderfully displayed, and their rage against God and against His people and the inhabitants of our world, will be more malignant, immediately preceding the Millennial dispensation of the church, than they have ever yet shewn themselves to be. The reason of this seems to be that they will, then, have only men in the flesh to operate upon, and that, too, only for a short time before their final expulsion from the earth. They will be no more permitted to accuse the saints of the Lord before him.

These remarks may open up a new train of thought to many readers of the Bible, and one which they may not have hitherto been disposed to look at, or to examine.—But it is time that God's people, yea, and the men of the world, in these latter days, should think more seriously on this subject. Satan has mighty power, and he will exert that power more and more as the day of his binding draws nigh. He will deceive all who dwell upon the earth to their final undoing if they flee not to Christ, as their only refuge. The exhortation of our Lord comes, therefore, with great force to every one, " Watch ye, therefore, and pray always, that ye may be accounted worthy to escape all these things that shall come to pass, and to stand before the Son of man."—Luke xxi : 36.

But, to return from this digression to our first parents in the garden of Eden.

Satan, failing in the object of his rebellion in heaven, came to earth and plotted the ruin of man. His plan was laid with consummate skill, and sad, indeed, to the world has been its success. Without entering now into any critical examination of the history of the fall of man, by the super-human wisdom of Satan, the facts themselves are plain enough for any one's comprehension. In carrying out his malicious design, Satan took possession of the body of an animal called the *Nachash;* in our version, the serpent. This animal was more subtle than any beast of the field which the Lord God had made. He selected the very best instrument that was to be found, for the accomplishment of his Satanic purposes. The animal either had the gift of speech originally from God, or when Satan took possession of its body, he spoke with an audible voice to the woman, and held a conversation with her through the medium of the animal. Her innocence of heart and purity of mind, or her ignorance, at that time, of the peculiar character of the animal, in its natural state, does not appear to have excited in her the least degree of surprise in hearing the animal speak to her, apparently, in a human voice, and in a language that she could understand. Some of the ancient Rabbins maintained that the *Nachash*, which was more wise or artful than every wild beast (micol chayath) of the field, was a creature of reason and understanding, and that it was formed like a human being, and

not as a reptile, or snake, which the waters produced.—
Moses arranges all the animals on earth in three classes,
viz. : the *Chayath*, the wild beasts; the *Behaimath*, the
tame beasts; and the *Remesh*, the creeping things. As
the *Nachash* was more wise, prudent or crafty (Heb. gna-
room) than all of the animals, they conclude that the animal used was one of the *ape* tribe, a species of baboon.—
The whole narrative accords better, they judge, with an
animal of that description than with a mere reptile. And
even now, in its degraded condition, it seems like a more
fitting instrument for Satan than a mere reptile. But,
leaving the particular nature and form of the animal out
of the question for the present, all agree that Satan, in
this plan of deception, concealed himself, and worked
through the instrumentality of the *Nachash*, whatever the
animal may have been.

From this inspired narrative we learn the following
facts, viz :

1. That Satan did take possession of the body of an
animal and kept it as long as he chose.

2. That he did so control the animal thus possessed by
him as to make it, for the time being, lose the distinctive
character which belonged to it, and to assume, in appearance, at least, that which belongs to another being.

3. That he did make an innocent and unfallen human
being imagine that she held converse with an animal, while
she actually was holding a conversation with Satan himself.

If he did so then, we are certainly justified in the conclusion that he can do so still, if God should permit him
to exert his power in that way. For we have no reason

to believe that Satan has less power, or craft, or malice now than he had then.

In the history of Job we have another inspired account of the power of Satan and of his hatred towards the good of the human race, and of his intense desire to do evil beyond what we may suppose he is ordinarily engaged in doing. From this account we learn the following additional facts, viz:

1. That Satan prompts men to acts of robbery and murder. He stirred up the evil passions of the Sabeans, and caused them to attack the servants of Job as they were peacefully ploughing in their field. They slew all the servants but one, and carried away the oxen and the asses.

2. He caused fire to fall from heaven, or rather he controlled the electricity which is in the clouds, causing the lightning to smite the servants who tended the sheep in the field, and killed all the sheep and all the men except one, who escaped to tell the sad news. Not only were the men and animals killed, but they were actually *burned up*. This is an effect which is never produced by the mere *stroke* of lightning in our days; or, if it be, it is exceedingly rare.

3. After exciting the Chaldeans to carry off the camels, and to kill the servants who attended them, he raised a storm in the wilderness that blew down the house in which the ten children of Job were assembled, and slew them all, and all the attendants on that occasion, except one, who was left to communicate the fact.

4. He laid his hand upon the body of Job, and smote him with a sore disease, so that, in the anguish of his soul, he longed for death to be freed from the bodily sufferings he then endured. His flesh became loathsome to himself.

His soul was scared with dreams, and terrified by visions and frightful appearance of horrid and unearthly things, so that he preferred strangling and death to life.

From this history we learn that, if God permit, Satan has power to control the winds and the electric fluid so as to overthrow dwellings, destroy property to any conceivable amount; to take away the lives of men, and of animals; to afflict the bodies of men with horrible diseases; to terrify the mind by the presentation to the imagination and to the eye of horrid and revolting sights; and to disturb the hours of sleep by harassing the mind with terrifying dreams, thus making life a burden, and forcing the unhappy sufferer to long for death, so as to be free from such torment. It also gives us an idea of the belief of Job as regards the influence of these things upon man after death. It is evident that he looked upon death as a guarantee that he would be freed from the influence of Satan's power forever. But if death gave him no release, why should he long for it? Satan is still the Prince of this world, and the Prince of the power of the air, and he still works in the hearts of the children of disobedience.

Not to occupy the attention of the reader any longer with the instances of Satan's power, as recorded in the Old Testament, we pass to those of the New Testament. Here we have a true and faithful record also of some of the wonderful workings of Satan. It is not our design to cite all these cases as given us by the inspired writers, though that might be profitable, but only a few as mere specimens of the whole, to show that the same mind originates them all, though the manifestations may be different. To any one, who is willing to receive the plain and unvarnished statements of the sacred writers, there can be no difficulty in accounting for all these wonders. Indeed, it requires no small amount of false reasoning to adduce even a plausible argument to show that the direct agency of Satan was not employed in their production.

Many suppose that the possessions in old times, were confined entirely to the Jewish people, and in a great degree to the times of our Lord. But this, certainly, is not the fact. They were found among the Gentiles also. The young woman, who had the spirit of Python (divination) as stated by Luke, Acts xvi: 11–20, was a Gentile. She was a Greek, and resided at Philippi, in Macedonia. We are sadly mistaken if we think that Satan has nothing to do with any body but the Jews. He has as warm friends, and as faithful servants, and as devout followers among the Gentiles as he ever had among the Jews. We do not think that the Gentiles need yield the palm to the Jews for fidelity to the cause of Satan. They certainly have nothing to lose in this respect, in comparison with their brethren.

As to the demoniacs being more abundant in the days of our Lord's incarnation, than at any other time before, or after it, cannot be proved, though the learned Joseph Mede, in his sermon on John x: 20, suggests that it was so. (See his works, p. 28. Ed. 1772.) The frequent accounts we have in the gospels of the doings of evil spirits, during the time of our Lord's ministry in Judea, is not owing to the fact, that they were any more busy in deceiving the souls of men, and in injuring their bodies then than in former times; but, it is owing to the fact, that we have there more recorded instances of the power of our Lord so signally displayed, in casting them out of men, women and children, than before, thus proving to the Jews, as well as to the Gentiles, that He was the true Messiah, the seed of the woman, and the promised King of Israel. We have no reason to believe that Satan does not now possess the souls and bodies of men in our world just as much as ever he did. God certainly is no better pleased with the corrupt workings of the human heart now than ever he was. And it will be a difficult thing to prove that the heart of the world, which is still at "enmity with God," is any more in love with holiness and purity and the glory of the Lord, than it was eighteen hundred years ago. Had we inspired information on this subject, we would, doubtless, find that multitudes of persons are now under the direct teachings and control of Satan and of evil spirits; and, that their conduct, which is in open violation of the laws of God, and of all the decencies and proprieties of life, and which is put down to the score of eccentricity of character, where ignorance, brutality, or native depravity of heart, should be accredited to Satan, the master spirit that rules and controls his wretched subjects at his will.

SATAN.

Satan is a personal existence and not a mere principle. He is an angelic being whom God created good as He did all things. But he sinned against God, and was cast down from the high position he once occupied. It would seem that pride was his sin.—1 Tim. iii. 6. But, how sinful feeling could first enter a holy heart we may never find out. The fact we do know. Satan did sin. What his name was before his sin we know not. This is his name since.

The word *Satan* means an adversary, an opposer. It is never found in the plural number, so that the sacred writers acknowledge but one Being of that name. He is styled by our Lord "The Prince of this world," (John xii : 3); by the Apostle, " The Prince of the power of the air," (Ep. ii : 2); and by the Jews, "The Prince of the demons," (Matt. ix : 34). The Septuagint translate the word *Satan* by the word *Diabolos*, which means an *Accuser*, a *Slanderer*. He is also called in the New Testament by a variety of names, indicative of his character and conduct, as Accuser, Destroyer, Liar, Murderer, &c. Nor is it any slander to say that he justly deserves them all.

The sacred writers and our Lord say there is a Devil, and but one. But, it is becoming the fashion now to deny his personal existence, to think that our Lord and the Apostles only spoke in accordance with the silly notions of those of their day, who supposed there was a being called Satan or the Devil, and that they themselves did not really believe in his existence. This is surely a progressive age—in unbelief of the word of God, at least, whatever else may stand still. But the very fact that the personal existence of Satan is denied by so many in our day, by many professing Christians, and a few who bear the name of ministers of Christ, as well as by those who deny the Word of God entirely, is to our mind one of the strongest proofs of the personal existence of such an Arch-Deceiver. This is one of what the Apostle calls "*ta bathe tou Satana*, the depths of Satan," (Rev. ii : 24). We can fully endorse the language of Dr. A. Clarke, who, speaking on the denial of Satan's existence, says: " Satan knows well that they who deny his being will not be afraid of his power and influence; will not watch against his wiles and devices; will not pray to God for deliverance from the

Evil One; will not expect him to be trampled down under their feet if he has no existence; and, consequently, they will become an easy and unopposing prey to the enemy of their souls. By leading men to disbelieve and deny his existence, he throws them off their guard. He is then their complete master, and they are led captive by him at his will. It is well known that among all those who make any profession of religion, those who deny the existence of the Devil, are they who pray little or none at all; and are, apparently, as careless about the existence of God as they are about the being of the Devil. Duty to God is with them out of the question, for those who do not pray especially in *private*, (and I never knew a devil-denier who did), have no religion of any kind (except the form) whatever pretensions they may choose to make."

One of the most striking proofs of the personal existence of Satan, which our times afford us, is found in the fact, that he has so influenced the minds of multitudes in reference to his existence and doings, as to make them believe that he does not exist; and that the hosts of Demons or Evil Spirits, over whom Satan presides as Prince, are only the phantacies of the brain, some halucination of mind. Could we have a stronger proof of the existence of a mind so mighty as to produce such results? Surely we have need to pray " Deliver us from the Evil One, *apo tou ponerou.*" Matt. vi : 13.

The word *Daimon*, in the New Testament, is usually rendered by one word Devil. But this is evidently improper, as it would lead us to believe that there are many devils, whereas there is and can be but *one*. And surely one is enough for any world; yea, one too many. Daimon in the New Testament always means an evil spirit, who is under Satan's control; a Demon. Ere long Satan will be cast out from this world, and with him all the host of demons, or evil spirits, who fell with him and who are under his control; then we shall have neither devil nor demon here.

NEW TESTAMENT POSSESSIONS.

In the gospels by Matt. viii: 28–33, Mark v: 1–16, and Luke viii: 26–36, we have a detailed account of two men who met our Lord when he came into the country of the Gergesenes, which lay on the east of the sea of Tiberias, in the land of Palestine. They were possessed with demons, *daimonizomenoi*. They had left the society of their friends and their homes, and took up their abode in the tombs.— These tombs (*mnemaia*) are very abundant in some parts of the Eastern world to this day. They are houses built over the graves of distinguished or wealthy persons by the governments of which they were honored members, or by their relatives. They are of different sizes and shapes.— Some of them are built square, others round, and from ten to thirty feet high. The most of those that are yet to be found in India were built by the Mohammedans. They are now used as dwellings or as stopping-places for travelers, being fitted up for these purposes. But formerly, no one dwelt in them—the friends of the deceased only visiting them occasionally as places of prayer. I have often lodged in these tombs while on missionary tours. We found them comfortable lodgings; and to those who are fond of retirement, they afford an agreeable resting-place. These men who met our Lord had been lodging in these tombs. They were exceedingly fierce; so much so that it was dangerous for any person to pass by the place where they were. The people of the country had often bound them with chains and fetters of ordinary strength, but they broke their chains, tore off all their clothing, and escaped, "being driven by the demon into the wilderness or desert places." Not only would they injure others, but they also injured themselves, cutting themselves with stones. No human power could subdue them. When they saw our Lord coming towards them they recognized him at once, and cried out in a loud voice, "Jesus, thou Son of God most High, what have we to do with thee? Art thou come hither to torment us before the time? We adjure thee by God that thou torment us not." And Jesus asked him, saying, "What is thy name?" And he said, "Legion;" for many demons had entered into him. They then besought our Lord that he would not cast them out into the bottomless pit or abyss—*eis ton abysson.*—Luke viii : 31; Rev. xx : 3. (The same Greek work is used in both these places); but that he would permit them to enter into the swine, some two thousand in number, that were feeding near the mountains a good way off. Our Lord commanded them to come out of the men, and giving them permission, they entered the swine, and so alarmed them that they all ran violently down a steep place into the sea, and were drowned. The men who kept the swine, when they saw what had happened to them, were alarmed, and fled into the city, telling everybody they met what had happened. In consequence of this news, the people, excited by curiosity, went out to see what had transpired. And when the people of the city saw the poor demoniac sitting at the feet of Jesus, clothed with proper garments that had been furnished him, and in the possession of his right mind, they felt afraid. But when the people of the country round about came and learned from those who had witnessed the scene, they felt differently. They were also taken with great fear, but their covetousness got the better of their benevolence. They thought only of the swine; and if Jesus would let all the demons enter them, the hope of their gains would be gone. Hence, they besought him most earnestly to depart, and leave them the demons and their swine. I doubt if they ever prayed so fervently before. Jesus heard their prayers, and left the country.— But the people of the city felt differently, for the demoniacs, at least one of them, was sent back to his own home by our Lord, with the commission to show to the people what great things God had done for him. He did so; and the people of the town who knew the poor possessed man, rejoiced with him in his deliverance. And when they heard that our Lord was about to return to the country, the people went out to meet him, and received him gladly. Such displays of the power of God now in saving sinners, would in many cases meet with similar treatment. There are multitudes now who would greatly prefer that Jesus should depart from their midst, rather than have him cast the evil spirits out of their neighbors, if by his doing so they should lose any of their swine or any of their unlawful gains. It is a blessed truth that all are not so.

In the gospel of Mark i : 23–26, we have an account of a man who was in the synagogue of the Jews in Capernaum, and who had an unclean spirit in him. (So these evil spirits do go to church sometimes.) When our Lord entered and began to expound the Word of God to the people, the man, or the spirit in him, cried out, saying, "Let us alone. What have we to do with thee, thou Jesus of Nazareth? Art thou come to destroy us? I know thee who thou art—the Holy One of God." "And Jesus rebuked him, saying, Hold thy peace, and come out of him. And when the unclean spirit had torn him, and cried with a loud voice, he came out of him. The people were amazed, and said, What thing is this? What new doctrine is this? for with authority He commandeth even the unclean spirits, and they do obey him."

The Evangelist Luke, who was a physician also, records the case of a woman, a Jewess, who had been bowed down by what he calls a spirit of infirmity (*pneuma astheneias.*) This was a different kind of spirit from those who were called "unclean," or "dumb," or merely evil, though they all were evil. The mode by which this spirit afflicted her was, probably, by curving her spine. Such was the effect of his power on her, that she could not lift herself up for the space of eighteen years! When our Lord saw her, he called her to him and said to her, "Woman, thou art loosed from thine infirmity!" And He laid hands on her, and she was made straight immediately, and glorified God. When the hypocritical ruler of the synagogue saw what had been done, he answered with indignation because the woman had been healed on the Sabbath day. Hypocrites are always great sticklers for forms and ceremonies, but pay very little regard to the soul and spirit of true religion. Our Lord reproved this hypocrite, telling him that if he himself would, as an act of mercy, on the Sabbath loose his ox or his ass, and lead the animal to a watering place where it might slake its thirst and save its life, so ought this daughter of Abraham, whom Satan had bound for *eighteen years*, be loosed from her bond on the Sabbath day.—Luke xiii: 11–17.

All that we say, at present, in reference to this case, is that it argues little for Luke's medical knowledge if he mistook the case and the nature of the disease; and as little for the veracity of our Lord if that disease and infirmity had not been produced by an evil spirit. The *hinder* is one thing and the *bond* is another; they cannot be the same.

There is but one case more of those recorded in the New Testament that I would refer to at present, and that is the case of that good woman, Mary Magdalene. The Evangelist Mark says that our Lord, after his resurrection, " appeared first to Mary Magdalene, out of whom he had cast seven demons."—Mark xvi : 9. They were demons, not diseases.

It is clear from this declaration that she had been greatly afflicted by evil spirits. Why this number took possession of her, the Bible does not say, and hence we do not know. There is, probably, no woman whose name is recorded in the Sacred Scriptures, whose character has been more slandered than that of Mary of Magdala. There seems to have been a special effort made to make her character so surpassingly vile, that the contrast in her conversion might be so much the greater, and that God thereby might get the greater glory. But the opinion that she was possessed by seven demons " on account of her wickedness," as Ambrose and Jansenius affirm, is without the least foundation in truth. She was no more to be blamed for being possessed by seven demons, than the man was out of whom a legion (five thousand) were cast, or the child who was possessed by but one. Jerome speaks favorably of her character and standing before her conversion. The probability is that she was a lady of great respectability and wealth in Galilee before her conversion, and that after it she was, next to the mother of Jesus, the most highly favored of women, for she was the *first* herald of a risen Redeemer. Andricomius says that "Magdalum was the castle of Mary Magdalene, where she was born and where she was healed." But it is the fashion for Protestants and Romanists to defame her character, and they will do it.— But surely it is bad enough to have her afflicted by seven real demons without being reproached for what she could not help, and charged with being what she was not. It is a pity that so many Christians allow themselves so easily to fall into sentiments based upon the loose remark of some old father in the church, who was probably no better than he ought to be in the very things he charges upon the innocent. When will the day come when the dogmas of men will be wholly set aside, and the Word of the Lord alone shall be the basis of thought and feeling, of word and of act? Lord, hasten the blissful day!

MODERN MANIFESTATIONS.

We enter now upon a most interesting part of our subject, viz; the consideration of spirit manifestations, as they are now witnessed in this land or in others. And here we must rely, in a great degree, upon the eyes and ears of others; for we have ourselves seen but few, comparatively speaking, of the many things that these spirits have done, and are yet doing in the midst of us. We have no disposition to call in question any of the facts which have been carefully and properly reported. Nor do we think that those who affirm that they have witnessed the phenomena which they describe, are mistaken, and that their senses of seeing, hearing and feeling have all deceived them. We cannot believe that they would affirm for truths, what they know to be false. It cannot be; for many of these witnesses are persons of undoubted veracity. They are men who would scorn to tell a lie on any account; and surely they could have no motive arising from worldly gain or approbation to do so. They are men of good sense, of sound and sane minds. Men of good judgment; men who can discriminate, as well as any others, between the true and the false; men who are in no way inferior to those around them, and whose testimony in a court of justice, on all subjects of which they have any personal knowledge, would be taken without the least hesitation. All this we say because we believe it. Among those who have witnessed these phenomena, are men in all the walks of life; men of science and of learning, physicians, judges, ministers, merchants, men of business in all the avocations of life, sober and sedate, as well as those who are of more excitable or enthusiastic temperament of mind. Surely, it cannot be that all these persons have been deceived as to all they have seen and heard. If the whole has been a mere trick, and if all these persons have been led to acknowledge phantasies for facts, then the wonder is a greater one still than that concerning which they testify.

There are, no doubt, many who, for the sake of gain, endeavor to impose upon the more credulous among the people, by base imitations of these phenomena. But the cheat can easily be detected by those who seek for the truth in the case. And the very fact itself that some attempt to imitate these wonders, proves that they are realities in the true sense of the word. Among those who claim a no higher character than that of mere mimics in these matters, we apprehend that there are none whose name or standing in society, would entitle them to any respect from others, while they have none from themselves. They are soon among the things that were. They even fall beneath contempt. They soon are out of mind.

But that persons of hitherto known respectability of character, of amiable dispositions, of moral worth, and of a godly life, and the firm believers in the truths of revelation, should suddenly rise up and proclaim to the world that things were done through them by a power outside of themselves, and in opposition to their own choice or will in the case, while at the same time, they attempted to practice deception upon the community, whose ears and eyes and senses were all awake to expose the cheat, if it be a cheat, and then demand of us faith in the reality of the things done, is asking of us a larger amount of faith than would be necessary to believe all the ghost-stories that have ever been published to the world since there was a pen to record them till now. Making all due allowance, then, for those who will lie, yet there are so many persons, both old and young, who cannot be deceived themselves, and who cannot possibly be attempting to deceive others, and who testify in the honesty of their hearts, to things they have heard and seen, we hesitate not to admit fully and freely the reality of all, each and every fact they state. The facts themselves however are one thing; the true explanation of them is another, and a very different thing. We seek the truth, and if we find it, we shall not fear to proclaim it; for "Truth is mighty, and must prevail."

A SCENE IN INDIA.

There are a few things which have come under our own observation, in connection with this subject, which we would now state. As to the facts themselves, we know that we were not deceived. Our explanation of them we shall give hereafter.

On the evening of Feb. 9th, 1834, about 6 o'clock, while standing in the door of Mr. Ropers' house in Aurungabad, India, I saw a crowd of people going towards a small Hindoo temple, which was in sight, and near at hand. On enquiry, I found that they were going to offer up two lambs in sacrifice to the god Vetal, the king of the demons, or in other words, to the Devil. In company with Mr. Roper and another gentleman, we followed the crowd. There were some forty persons in all, including the women and children. It was a family sacrifice, and was to be offered in fulfillment of a vow. A few persons playing on instruments of music, such as are used on these occasions, led the way. Then followed two men bringing the lambs for sacrifice. The one was carried on the shoulders of one of the men: the other was led. Both of them were decorated with garlands of flowers. After these followed a person, carrying the sacred fire, and next in order the families concerned. When they arrived at the temple, which was a small building, some twelve or fifteen feet square, the people bowed down before the idol, which was within and opposite the door, and then walked round the temple twice. A lamp was then lit from the sacred fire and placed in the temple immediately before the idol. The person who officiated on this occasion was a priestess, with a wild look, disheveled hair, and with garments that needed washing. Her dress was the usual dress of the Hindoo women in that part of the country, viz., the *cholee*, or body dress, a kind of spencer, the sleeves reaching only to the elbows; and the *loogurda*, a garment wrapped round the waist and extending below the knee. On the left sleeve of her dress, small patches of red flannel had been sewed to represent the small-pox, which she professed to be able to cure. She was assisted by a man, the counter-part of herself in appearance. The priestess then marked the foreheads of all the people with red paint, such as was on the idol. Having washed her hands in clean water, she took a handful of the small branches of the *kurdoonimb*, the bitter-lime-tree, and tied them together in the form of a broom. This she held in her hand while her assistant poured upon it a vessel full of water. While engaged in washing these branches she continued to mutter something in a low and rapid tone of voice, which no one could distinctly hear, and to which no one seemed to pay any attention. This being over, she ordered her assistant to wash the head and forelegs of one of the lambs with water, into which she had thrown some salt and some of those bitter leaves. The head of the lamb was next marked with the red paint. Some of the bitter leaves and salt were given it to eat, but it refused them. Its mouth was opened and some of the salt and water and another fluid, (but what I could not learn,) were forced down its throat. This seemed to stupify the animal, so that being let loose, it staggered about among the people. After a few minutes, one of the company gave it a gentle tap on the side of the head, which caused it to turn its face towards the door of the temple. As soon as this was done, the sacrificer seized it, threw it forcibly on its left side, the head being towards the door, and immediately cut off its head and the right leg at the knee. These were moved up and down before the idol, and then placed before the door of the temple. When the lamb had ceased to move, it was dragged to one side, where it was left. All this time the priestess stood by and was muttering something to herself. She now stepped forward to the blood, holding the little bundle of branches over it in her hand, and while the sacrificer poured water on it, she sopped it in the water and the blood, and proceeded to sprinkle all the people in the blood of the sacrifice, having first sprinkled the idol and the doorposts of the temple. When she came to us, as we stood at the end of the semi-circle of the crowd, she stopped and frowned, as if considering whether to sprinkle us or not. Then going to the door of the temple, she stood gazing in upon the idol, and while she continued her muttering, the brush dropped from her hand. She started back, and in a frantic like manner began to jump and scream and pull her hair. On a sudden she was seized with trembling through her whole body—her arms were extended—her mouth was wide open, and her eyes rolled from side to side. Again she jumped, and groaned, and raved, and screamed, and finally was thrown back full length as if lifeless to the ground. Her fall was broken by two of the women present, who sprang forward and broke her fall, which, if they had not done, it seems to me, it would have knocked her own or some other spirit out of her, and brought her to her senses; or, at least, must have injured her much. After lying on the ground stretched out for some time apparently lifeless and stiff, she began to move, rose up slowly and gradually, and resumed her former appearance. She then addressed the people and told them that the god had accepted their sacrifice. This being ended, one of the company paid her a few *pice* (a small copper coin less than the value of our cent,) for her services; the musicians struck up their music; the company formed in a line and returned back to their homes.

Finding the old lady pretty calm in mind, and looking intently at the money she had just received, I approached her, and began to enquire about the sacrifice and the meaning of what I had witnessed. But, whether she thought that our design was to injure her, or in some way to molest her, we know not; she kept silent; and when urged to speak, she began to whine, and pretended to be afraid of us, as perhaps she was. Gaining no information from her, we left her. From the assistant we merely learned the additional fact that, while the god was pleased with the honor conferred on it, so were they with what they had received, two lambs and some money.

I need hardly say that the whole scene interested me exceedingly at the time. The fact that the lambs were *without blemish;* that they were brought to the *door* of the temple (their tabernacle); that *salt* and bitter herbs were used; that the head and foreleg were *waved* before the idol; that the idol, the doorposts of the temple, and the people, were sprinkled with the *blood* of the sacrifice; and that the lambs were left for the use of the priestess, and the attendants on the temple—all tended to show that sacrifices, as they now exist among the Hindoos, must have had their origin in imitation of those appointed by the Lord and practiced by Israel.

But in reference to this whole matter, and especially the ravings and the contortions and convulsions of the possessed, I would say, that the universal opinion of the people is, that they are wholly *involuntary* on their part. Their idea is that the god, which they say dwells in or near the idol, and to which the sacrifice is offered, and which, as in the present case, comes out of the idol and takes possession of the woman, through her speaks to the people, giving them the information they may need. The Hindoos fully believe that the god which is a demon or evil spirit, does take possession of the bodies of individuals. Whatever the person may do in that state of frenzy, is considered as the act of the god, and not of the person possessed. That the Devil does now, at times, possess people, is the firm faith of all the Mohammedan population. The Hindoos believe that the same effects are produced by their *Rackshus*, or evil spirits. The priests have their fixed rules, by which they profess to determine the question whether the possession be a real one or not. If it be real, according to their rules, then the person thus possessed, may be worshipped for the time being as the god itself. They do oftentimes worship the Devil. They pray to him, they ask him to take possession of them. And is it unreasonable to suppose that their prayers in this matter may be answered? That there is any trick on the part of these possessed ones, seems to be impossible. The natives who look on give them credit for honesty, at least, in the matter; and those who are Christians, who have witnessed them, so far as I have known their views, agree in the fact that they are veritable possessions. Probably every missionary in India has witnessed something of the same kind. The reader will find a short and interesting article on the subject in Rev. Dr. Allen's work on "India, Ancient and Modern," p. 384.

In conversing recently with a missionary from India, he mentioned two instances of demoniacal possessions which came under his own observation. One was that of a boy in one of the schools at Bombay. While the missionary was in the school, and giving instruction to the youth assembled, one of the lads was seized and thrown down upon the floor: he began to groan, and foam at the mouth, and was thrown about in a most singular manner. The missionary went towards him to raise him up. The boys cried out, "Bhootagrust, Sahib;" that is, "He is possessed." After some time, they carried him home.

One of the Hindoo converts, before her conversion, had been grievously tormented by the demons. After she had become a Christian, and had united herself to the church, one of her acquaintance asked her if the "Bhoots," the demons, troubled her now. She replied, "I believe now in Jesus, and they don't come near me any more."

Now, whatever others may think on the subject, one thing is certain, she really believed that she had been, and that, too, for years tormented by demons; and it is presumed that she should know; but after she had embraced the truth, as it is in Christ, and placed her hopes and trust in Him, the evil spirits left her. We have her views of her own case. Was she mistaken? Are we sure she was not right as to what had been the matter with her?

As to the boys in the school, they had no doubt of the fact that their young companion was possessed by a demon. We state these cases merely to show what the opinion of the people is on this subject. Others may attribute it all to the effect of imagination, or to simple disease. But can they prove that that disordered imagination, or that disease by which the person may be afflicted, is not itself the production of an evil spirit? But of this we will speak again.

It is evident from the statements of travelers from the various parts of the heathen world, that the belief in spirits, distinct from man in the flesh, is, generally speaking, prevalent among the people. Not only do the people believe that they do exist, but these spirits can also take possession of the bodies of men. There may be, and doubtless is, much superstition connected with the faith of the people on these subjects; but still, their faith has its foundation in truth. The Old and New Testament writers speak of the existence of such evil spirits and influences, and we have no reason to think that they have yet been wholly expelled from the abodes of men.

The Rev. Joseph Wolff, the missionary to the Jews, and of world-wide fame, in his published account of his travels through Bokhara, Affghanistan, and India, gives us the views of the people of Cashmere and others on the subject, and also his own. He was charged by Lieut. Burnes with having cast a demon out of some godless Mohammedan somewhere near Cabool, and this was considered proof positive that the honored missionary was insane. When Mr. Wolff was with me in Philadelphia, I asked him particularly about the matter. The account he gave me was substantially this : He said that one evening while sitting in a tent with some Mohammedans and others, and discussing subjects in reference to the character of Jesus of Nazareth, and the plan of salvation by him, a Mohammedan cried out and interrupted their conversation by such unearthly groanings, and language, and actions, that being fully convinced that he was possessed by an evil spirit, Mr. W. turned to him, and fixing his eyes upon him, said, " In the name of the Lord Jesus of Nazareth, the Messiah, I command thee to be silent !" and immediately the man was silent. He became calm, and continued so during the remainder of the interview. Others may form their own opinion of the matter, but the united opinion of Mr. W. and the company with him was, that the man was a demoniac, and just such as we read of in the New Testament.— We may be mistaken, but we think it will be found that the most of our Christian missionaries who have labored for any length of time in any part of the heathen world, have witnessed such scenes as correspond very well with the scriptural account of demoniacal possessions. And if they are not in reality demoniacal possessions, which the people themselves believe they are, it will be difficult to account for them on any other theory.

WITCHCRAFT.

Since the entrance of the Evil One into our world, the evidences of his power and evil workings are abundant.— In every land you find them. They are in every age, and among all nations. None are exempt. Our own country has not escaped. Satan does not need the assistance of steam power to transport himself or his angels from one land to another. He visited America long before the introduction of machinery, by which our sluggish bodies may be carried from place to place. He is the Prince of the power of the *air*—and although not omnipresent nor omniscient, yet he has agencies constantly at work, so that his influence is felt, and constantly too, throughout the world.

There are but few in our country now who have not read or heard something of the cruel hunt after witches and wizards (or, in the improved language of the present day, *mediums*) in England, Scotland, Sweden, and America, from the year 1640 down to 1692, or later, and of the sad results of that movement, both here and there. After two hundred years have rolled away, we of this day may suppose that we understand these matters better than the learned of that day. Perhaps we do. But after all, can we give a satisfactory solution of those sad operations without referring them, at least in some degree, to something more than mere wild imaginings or unrestrained fanaticism? We are astonished now to see the names of the great men of that age, in all those countries and here also, judges, governors, jurors, ministers, and people, learned and influential, all uniting in condemning to death, hanging, drowning, and torturing men, but especially helpless women and children, because the people believed that they were under the influence of Satan; and some of them, to save their lives, by confession, declared they were. It is truly sad to think of the cold-blooded and deliberate murders that were then committed under the sanction of law, and for the honor, as they thought, of the religion of Jesus, that proclaims peace and good will to men. We fully believe the testimony of Scripture in reference to the wickedness of the heart of man by nature. But bad as the human heart is, we do not believe that it is so bad as to act, as we know it did during that reign of witch-terror, without aid and assistance from without—even from Satan himself. We doubt not that many of those unhappy victims were under Satanic influence, and that too, like the poor demoniacs of old, without any will or wish of their own. But we also believe, and have fully as much evidence, if not more in the case, that the judges and jurors, the ministers and the people, who engaged in that unrighteous work of condemning and executing so many of their fellow-beings, were themselves under the direct influence of the Devil.— They had the power in their own hands; and hence, they saved their own lives. Satan raised the storm, and kept it up and controlled it so as to accomplish the object he had in view, namely, the ruin of many, and the bringing a reproach upon the religion of Christ, through its professed adherents, whom he himself had possessed. If there be guiltiness in the matter, and no doubt there is, we judge it is not to be chargeable so much to those who were *involuntarily* the subjects of those delusions as to those who lent themselves, as the willing servants of Satan, for the time being, in persecuting and killing those who needed rather their prayers and their sympathies, and especially deliverance from the power of the Devil by the grace of God.

At the present time, we have in this country the manifestations of Satanic influence, which are neither "few nor far between." They may be arranged under two general classes, viz. :

1. Those which are more immediately connected with the moving of material objects ; and—
2. Those which exhibit a mind in connection with them, and controlling them.

As to the first of these—viz., the movements of material objects—we have published accounts of them, which, if particular cases be necessary, are sufficient to satisfy any reasonable mind of their reality; for we have them in any reasonable quantity and variety.

Having already stated that we have no reason to call in question the truth of many of these published accounts, as to the facts themselves, we hesitate not to refer to them as facts. As to the explanation of those facts, we express no opinion here : we reserve that for another place.

Taking then the statements which are given us by multitudes of individuals over their own signatures, and whose testimony we do not venture to question, we have the movement of tables by persons laying their hands upon them, and rappings, and noises in any conceivable quantity. So far as we learn, the mode of operation is this. A few sit at a table, one of whom must be a medium ; that is, if we understand the term, a connecting link between the visible and invisible ; and one, through whom the invisible agent may work. They lay their hands upon it ; they sit in silence, and in due time the table begins to move. At first the table was spoken to as an intelligent being, and asked sundry questions, according to the fancy of the questioner. These would be answered by tilting up and down. One tilt is no ; two are doubtful, and three are yes. The table was then asked to stand on one foot, and it would do so; to walk about, and to answer all sorts of questions. All of which, whether the answers were right or wrong, seemed to please the operators, and the spectators much Afterwards the questions were put, and are now put, when these things are done, to the invisible agent who, it is said, moves the table. The form now is—" Will the spirit tell us ;" or, if a name be given, " Will M. or N. answer our question ?" So that now the intercourse is held between the living, and the invisible, through a mere table. It was said at first, by nearly all, and by many yet, that all this is the effect of electricity, or of the operation of one of the minds present.

But here is a table on which no hands are laid. It is requested to rise, or the spirits are requested to raise it up for the gratification of those present. It does rise, and does remain suspended in the air. No hand touches it; no trick has done it. But it is done. Here, so far as human eyes can see, the laws of gravitation are suspended, or in some way overcome, so that the table does remain suspended in the air. Does electricity or magnetism also do that ? What law of nature is there, so far as we know them, by the observance of which any one, or any number of men can, by the mere force of their will, order a table to rise and remain suspended in the air, and it will obey them?

But, this is not all. Not only are tables moved, and other portions of matter lifted up, and moved about and are broken to pieces; persons are lifted up without any visible agency, and are carried bodily from one room to another, and from place to place: persons unskilled in music, even little children, have played well and skillfully on instruments of music without having learned a note, and the instruments themselves have played while no hand touched them; hands have appeared writing on walls; they have been felt; some of them apparently warm and others cold to the touch; persons have been seized and shaken, and their garments torn; they have been tossed about; the form of bodies known to be long dead have been made to appear; secrets have been revealed and facts have been made known, which were beyond the reach of man to find out: friends have been represented as coming back from the invisible world, and holding converse with the living, some times speaking words of comfort, and at others words of warning, in many cases words of truth, and in others words of falsehood.

A friend of mine in whose eye-sight and statements I have every confidence, states the following facts among others.

One day happening to pass by the door of a friend, he called him to him; after the usual salutations of the day, the following conversation in substance passed between them—

"Have you witnessed any of these table-tippings which

are talked about so much?" (they had just begun to be known in Philadelphia then.)

"We know but little about them," he replied.

"We can turn the tables in our house—our little daughter can do it easily; but we can't do it without her: come in and see."

They went in, and in due time were seated in an upper room. The father, mother, and little daughter, some fourteen years of age, sat by the little table. Their hands were laid upon it. All looked on. After a few minutes, sure enough the table tipped up. The father then asked, how many persons are there in the room; how many windows are there to the room: a coin was held out in the closed hand —the kind and date were asked, also the several ages of the persons present; to all these the answers were correct. It was then suggested, perhaps the little girl can write also. A pencil was placed in her hand, and soon it began to move. Several questions were asked her, and answers were given which seemed to gratify the father and interest him very much. Finally the question was put, "who moves her hand?" Immediately, in large distinct letters, she wrote the word "Devil." When she lifted up her pencil and saw the word she had written, she dropped the pencil, and a shudder passed over her that shook her whole frame. She evidently felt afraid, and her parents were silent. They looked amazed. At length the father said, "I guess we had better stop now." That ended the interview. But, the conclusion that our friend drew from what he saw was, that there must have been a mind different from any one then present, controlling her hand, for no one had suggested that name, and surely the little girl herself had not intended to write the word. What led her to do it? That is the question.

On another occasion, the same friend was walking down one of our streets, and seeing a small second hand bookstore, he stepped in to look at the odd volumes that were there. He saw among them a work on Spiritualism, which led him to make a remark on the subject of the book. This led to a conversation with the bookseller on the subject. In the course of conversation, he said there was a lady then in his house, who did some strange things. He immediately left the store and called her. She came into the store and sat down on a chair near the counter. He gave her an alphabetical card. She laid it down before her, and placed her hands upon it. Her eyes soon closed. She then bandaged her eyes, and reversed the card. He asked her sundry questions. Her hand immediately was shaken violently, and she rapidly spelled out an answer to each question, by placing the fore finger upon each letter in regular order. After the experiments were over, the lady was asked what she thought about the whole matter. She replied, that she did not know what to think about it. The influence came upon her suddenly, about a year ago—her hand is moved against her will, and she has no knowledge of what she has spelled out, or the meaning of any thing done unless it be told her by those who may witness it.

Our friend was perfectly satisfied that the lady, (who is married and a mother), was honest in all that she said. She makes no gain by it. The whole thing is strange to her, she cannot account for it, and only when among her friends, does she now submit to have her hand moved for the gratification of others. He is of the opinion that there is a mind different from hers, that controls her hand on these occasions.

We would mention but one more case which our friend witnessed. It was this: In company with another friend, he went to see a person who it is said becomes entranced (we think that is the term used.) Having entered the house, they were conducted to an upper room where the lady and her mother were. A small table was brought out and placed in the middle of the room, and she and they sat near it. She laid her hands upon it, and then asked if there were any spirits present. The answer was, Yes.— Are they good? Yes. To what sphere do you belong? The sixth. Will you take possession of the medium? Yes. How soon? In three minutes.

All now was quiet. In a minute's time her eyes closed, her arms began to twitch; her whole body began to be agitated; her face was contorted; she moaned, and a peculiar sensation was produced about the neck and throat, as if swallowing something; her hands became perfectly rigid, and her arms were stretched out. In three minutes' time her muscles relaxed; she was again calm and composed, and spake out, saying, "I am happy." It was asked, "Who are you?" "I am Sarah J. I lived in Ohio, and died six years ago. I was a member of the church; I lived a Christian life; I am progressing rapidly." To various questions proposed to her, she said she believed in Jesus as she did while on earth, but in many things her views were changed. There was punishment there for the bad, but all might make an atonement for their sins by suffering; and all would finally enter higher and happier spheres. Some were a long time in getting out of the lower ones, which were places of torment. She said she saw the wicked a great way off; they were quarreling with each other, and some evil one was taunting them. She felt happy in being able to come back and tell to others her joy and her peace. She had but a short time to stay; she must go. A pause ensued, the twitching again returned, and a slight moan or two was heard, and she opened her eyes.

On inquiring if she knew what she had been speaking about, she said, No; she had no knowledge of it whatever. She felt no pain from the spasms or the process of the possession.

Shortly after the influence came upon her again, and she passed through a similar process. Finally, while sitting calmly with her hands on the table, she asked if there were any spirits present who would take possession of her. The table gave three violent raps. Her mother, who sat by, said, "That's a bad spirit;" and seemed unwilling that her daughter should be made the subject of its control.— But she wished it. Immediately she was most violently shaken, and gave several deep groans, and her features were much contorted; her whole countenance was changed. In a moment more she spoke out: "Oh, cursed passion! He provoked me to do it!" "Who are you?" "I am the murderer of Parkman. Oh, oh! I did it;" and she shuddered all over. "What did you do it for?" "He kept asking me for the money." "Did you hate him?" "No; I had no intention of doing it until he came and asked me again for it. Oh, oh! I killed him." "Where did you strike him?" "Oh, here," laying her hand on the back part of her head. "Oh, oh!" and she gave a deep groan. "What did you do with him?" "I dissected him—oh! I did." "Are you sorry for it now?" "Oh, oh! I can't repent—I can't." "Is there then no hope for you?"—

"I have just heard that there is; but the time is so far off before I shall begin to progress. Oh, I can't repent.— Oh, oh!" and then she became violent. She pounded the table with her fists and knuckles, so that, fearing she might break some of her bones, our friend interposed his arm, so that she might spend her strength on it. But that not being very pleasant, he drew his arm back, and pulled away the table from her. She rose and caught hold of it, pulling it back, and pounded it more furiously, and as rapidly as her hands could well move. All the time her features were distorted, and the very picture of rage and despair. There seemed to be no stopping or calming her. All became somewhat alarmed. Her mother also seemed so. She arose and caught hold of her daughter, and spoke out aloud—"In the name of the Lord, I beseech you to leave her!" In a moment she sat down. She groaned once or twice, and then opened her eyes, and looked round and asked what was the matter. She seemed to be bewildered. When told what had happened, she said she thought that some bad spirit had had possession of her, but she had no knowledge of what had transpired. "But did you not hurt your hands by pounding so hard?" "No," she replied. "But did I not hurt you?" "Yes, but not much. We wished," he said, "to save you from being injured."

Having seen enough at that time, she was requested not to permit any more of the spirits to take possession of her if she could prevent it. Astonished at what he saw, after a few minutes' conversation with the family he came away. He learned, however, from the young woman, that according to her account her father died many years ago, a wicked man; that after some years in the invisible world, and after suffering a great deal, he obtained permission (from whom she did not say) to come back to this world and make a medium of his daughter. By doing so he had done a good act, and that helped him to make some progress towards being better and happier.

This is the account she gave of the matter; but she does not attempt to explain or account for the influence that came upon her some two years ago. She professes to feel as yet no injury from the agitations and shakings she has to pass through. When asked if she really thought that the spirits that took possession of her were what they professed to be—viz., the spirits of departed human beings, her father's spirit among them—she said she thought so, but was not certain; still, that seemed to be her belief of the matter.

As to the above account, we can have no doubt of the reality of the events themselves, for our friend saw them, and could not be mistaken. Indeed, there are so many eye and ear witnesses to so many of these phenomena, that it is vain to deny the things themselves.

But here is another account, and with this we shall conclude this part of the subject. We cut it, a few weeks ago, out of one of the papers of the day. The statement is as follows:

THE PHENOMENA AT DAVENPORT'S.

"We have on various occasions alluded to the mysterious and inexplicable manifestations at the above locality on Maine street, which are being daily and nightly developed, and of a character to startle the most intelligent minds in this or any other community. That these demonstrations partake of more than mere human agency, we are inclined to think any reasoning mind, after fairly looking into the matter, and bringing all ordinary and extraordinary talent to bear upon it, and failing to elucidate, will be obliged to acknowledge, we cannot for a moment doubt; but of the character of the cause which does produce phenomena so peculiar, it is not our province to speculate upon.

It would appear that mind, the concentrated mental force present at certain times, will either in the one case help to produce certain effects, or in other cases serve to destroy them. Also, that the atmosphere at times is favorable or unfavorable, and other influences operating for or against the demonstration of a new and most mysterious principle, the germ of which is now beginning to manifest itself. Night after night, and daily, also, can be heard a voice, which speaks with, to say the least, human strength, and conveying ideas often of more than ordinary human sagacity. This intelligence can be communicated with when one is alone with the single medium, a boy of some twelve years old, whose hands are held, at which time the air is filled with noises, and sounds partaking of voices, whistlings, fingering of the strings of violins, guitars, &c.

Last evening, with a number of respectable and perfectly sensible observers, we witnessed all of the above demonstrations, and a few more of even greater mystery. Lights of a character resembling shooting stars, or the rapid passage of lightning, filled the room for several minutes. This phenomena is, we are told, often observed when human and atmospheric influence permit; but a still more unaccountable demonstration was given of this superhuman power. There were two mediums at the table, the eldest a lad of sixteen, we should judge. This boy was lifted, chair and all, to the ceiling, a distance of some twelve feet, at least, and struck heavily there, indenting the plastering, and marking the chair with the whitewash. A request was made to the invisible agent who controls and converses with them, to do it again, and permit the boy to mark the ceiling with red chalk. After the company satisfied themselves that, by placing a chair on the table, and standing up in it, the boy could not reach the ceiling within several feet, the lights are put out, and immediately a heavy body, like dropping a hundred weight upon the floor, was felt to have come down; the light was produced, and a red chalk line on the ceiling showed where the boy had been.

Perhaps some rational explanation can be given of human agency in all this; if so, we should like to get hold of it. We feel that ordinary principles known to man, will not admit of it; but what is it? There we will leave the subject."—*Buffalo Republican.*

The question now arises, in view of all these and of other facts that might be stated, and which the reader may find in the published books of the spiritualists, and which receive their full approbation; what is the proper explanation of them? Are they all mere tricks, or are they natural phenomena, or are they supernatural? And if so, what kind of agency produces them?

CHAPTER III.

THE THEORIES.

ADMITTING then all the facts that have hitherto been reported in connection with these various forms of spiritual manifestations, to be veritable facts, the question arises, how are they to be explained? Every effect must have an adequate cause. This is common sense and sound philosophy. There is a cause for all these effects. What is that cause?

TRICKERY.

To this question it is answered by some, the whole thing is a *trick;* a mere matter of deception, and of lies on the part of those who are the actors, or mediums, in the case. It is a plan to gain money or notoriety.

To such remarks, so unguarded, and so devoid of truth, we reply, those who make them know not what manner of spirit they are of: they know not what they say, nor whereof they affirm. In all probability they are made by those who have never carefully examined the subject, and who think the shortest way and the best to treat any and every delusion by which souls may be ruined, for time and for eternity, is by a sneer and by assumed contempt. We have heard such arguments from the pulpit, against spiritualism, and can only say, that, if we had the least bearing toward the delusion, or had doubts as to its true character such preaching would rather make a convert of us to it, than give us a more perfect abhorrence of it than we have. It is an utter impossibility that the multitudes of men, women, and little children, who are now the subjects of these manifestations, and many of them without any wish or will on their part, can be practicing trickery and falsehood. That some few may do so can easily be supposed. That this is the case with any great number cannot be; and any one, who is acquainted with the facts in the case, and the persons who are engaged in it, must know that it cannot be that they are deliberately trying to deceive the people. We give them full credit for honesty at least.

It has been said, that all the noises and rappings that have been heard, could be produced by a person, whose knee-joints could, at will, be made to crack!! Others have thought that wires or springs, or something of the kind, had been previously arranged by the operators, and that the noises were produced in that way. These were among some of the first guesses at explanation; but no one now, we believe, thinks that these come any way near to the truth. These explanations are wholly discarded.

VENTRILOQUISM

Was next supposed to be the true explanation of the sounds and noises. From what we heard about the matter, at first, we supposed that it might be so : for these abdominal talkers can do many very strange things, and all too, they tell us, quite scientifically. But this will not account for the noises heard, when there is no one within speaking distance to produce them. They have been heard at such times, and places, and under such circumstances as wholly to forbid the idea of their proceeding from any ventriloquist, however great his power may be.

We have witnessed the jugglers in India perform some astonishing things, and have heard of others still more unaccountable having been performed by them, and which they said were all a mere series of tricks, and could be done by any one else, if they had the tact and the knowledge. We doubt it. We are by no means certain that there is not assistance lent these persons by a power outside of themselves. They may think it is all from themselves; but we believe they are mistaken.

But, from the curious tricks that some may perform in the presence of others, and the mode of doing these things at the time, so that they cannot possibly be detected, the conclusion is drawn, that all these rappings, voices, noises, music, &c., are of a like character. The whole is scientifically done, and there is really nothing wrong, but only amusement in the whole matter! Ventriloquism cannot possibly explain the phenomena.

ELECTRICITY,

Galvanism, odic-force, and the power of the human will, have all been brought forward to account for the wonders of spiritualism. The French philosophers, who, of course, are presumed to know everything that appertains to the mysterious, have written learnedly upon the subject. So have learned and scientific men in this country done the same thing. They had it all right. Yes, they know all about it. But soon some new manifestation was made, and then the books which they had written on the subject, and their finely argued-out theories too were all cast overboard into

THE THEORIES—ELECTRICITY—GALVANISM.

the wide sea of uncertainty, where many a favorite theory on many a subject lies quietly asleep.

Electricity and galvanism could do, as agencies, when directed by some mind, many wonderful things. But these wise men soon found that electricity would not cause a lamp to be lifted up off the mantle, and be dashed into a looking-glass worth some $50 or more; or the door of a room to be locked on the inside, while no one was in the room; or garments to be torn off persons while they have been quietly sitting in their room; or when persons had knelt down to pray, to pull them off their knees; or when papers were placed in private drawers in writing desks, and locked up, that they should be torn to pieces, or fire be kindled in them, so that they were actually burnt up, and the wood of the desk charred; or that persons should be pushed about and injured, and when no body was in or near the house, that the doors should still remain locked, and the drawers too, and yet all the clothes be taken from the drawers, and strewed about over the floor, or dressed up in all kinds of fantastic shapes;. or that persons should be lifted up, and carried forward for squares without their feet touching the ground; or that the persons could rise up in public assemblies, and speak intelligibly, and scientifically, and philosophically, for an hour at a time on subjects they knew but little of, and when the discourse was over did not know what had been said, and could by no means use language so fine, so chaste, and so appropriate; or could dictate and write letters, and drop them down in a room as if they had fallen from the ceiling, while the ink was still wet on the paper; and all these things and thousands of others that have been done, they found were actually done, and that their electricity, though it could rive the oak and plough the earth in deep furrows, and fire the ship on the sea, or the house on the land, when permitted by God to do its work, yet it could not do, by man's control, these small things. Electricity now has got permission to retire from the field of spiritualistic wonders. The leave of absence, we think, is just, and demanded by the nature of the case.

THE HUMAN WILL.

This has been brought, in the next place, to bear upon the subject, and to explain it. Much has been said about the voluntary and involuntary powers and instincts of the human mind. But, in all our life, we have never yet read, or heard of a case where a man, by taking thought, by his intense anxiety of mind, or fixedness of thought, or purpose of will could, or ever did add one cubit to his stature, or prolong his life an hour; or even change the color of a hair, making it either white or black. (Mat. v: 36; vi: 27.) If so small a thing as that cannot be done by the force of the human will; on what ground can we expect that these greater things can be done? We know that the will of some men may be called an iron will, and may, by its firmness, produce many mighty effects, by swaying the minds of others; but, all the force of all the minds of men from Adam down to the present time, if they could be brought to bear unitedly upon any piece of dead matter, could never move it an inch, much less lift up heavy masses of matter, and hurl them about as chaff before the wind. It is not the province of the human mind to do such things. Its field of operation, and its work is different. It also has a free permit to withdraw from this spirit-work, and work when and where the Lord appoints.

By universal consent, all who are known as Spiritualists have given up the idea that these phenomena are produced by any thing else than by

THE SPIRITS OF DEPARTED HUMAN BEINGS.

They may not have always thought so. But, it is evident, that this is now the theory. They profess to believe that the spirits of all persons, immediately after death, enter into the invisible world, (which is all around us,) with the same moral character which they had while in the body. If they are wicked, they enter the second sphere, the space which is immediately around the earth. Here are none but what are called undeveloped spirits. They retain all their ignorance, and rudeness, and all their characteristic traits of character while on the earth and dwelling among the living in the flesh. In this, and in all the spheres, there are many circles, probably seven. So that a spirit that is bad must enter one of these seven circles of this second sphere. Development and progression are the established order of the invisible world. Many of the spirits are so bad that it is a long time before they begin their progressive course upwards. But sooner or later this is the case. In this place they make an atonement for the sins they had committed in life, and of which they had not repented. When they once begin to rise, their progress may be very rapid. And, as they will henceforward continue to make progress, they will all ultimately be perfectly and eternally holy and happy.

Those who are good persons on earth will, at their death, enter into a higher sphere. Here they enjoy the society of the good. The spirits in the higher spheres can hold intercourse with the good even in the spheres above them.

All of these spirits, both the good and the bad, are anxious to re-enter the bodies of persons still in the flesh. The good spirits aim to do good, and their desire is to instruct mortals in the right way, and to correct the many erroneous views which persons, in the flesh, fall into by their implicit belief in the statements of the Bible. The Bible, these spirits say, is wrong in many of its statements. It is their object to correct these errors, if possible. Hence their great desire to enter the bodies of living human beings, so as to communicate these things to the world. It is not every one that they can control, or fit for their service, so as to communicate by them. But, they can prepare them for these communications by a process of training, that may continue for a longer or shorter period of time. These persons are called

MEDIUMS.

There is a great variety of mediums. Some are called writing mediums: others are speaking, or seeing, or healing mediums. The modes of communication with mortals in the flesh, through these different mediums, by the spirits of the departed are various, but the agents are the same— they are always the spirits of the departed.

The bad spirits are equally desirous to communicate with men in the flesh, or rather to enter into the body of some one living, so as to get some respite from their suffering in the lower spheres. They also retain the same tempers in the spirit world that they had while here. As they were fond of quarreling and strife while here, so the desire to get where they can indulge again their old practice of disputation, and wrangling, urges them to take possession of any body that they can possibly enter. They are not choice of the persons they may enter, nor are they in any way particular as to the propriety of their conduct while they have possession of the body. They often make the person possessed by them, use filthy language and gestures to correspond to their words.—These are what may be called unclean spirits—or dirty spirits. Truth is, by no means, sacred with them. They will utter falsehoods, and tell you to your face that it is their business to lie—these are lying spirits. All of these spirits, both the good and the bad, are, according to Spiritualism, the souls of departed human beings; for they maintain that there is no devil, and of course there are no evil angels, as Christians generally believe.

TEACHINGS OF THE SPIRITS.

There is an old proverb that says, "As he (man) thinketh in his heart so is he," Prov. xxiii: 7. This statement is founded in truth; for a man's thoughts are a good index to the state of his heart. There is another statement equally true, of this nature : " Out of the abundance of the heart the mouth speaketh," Matt. xii : 34 : and yet another which says, " Ye shall know them by their fruits," Matt. vii : 16. As all these statements are admitted truths, it seems to be perfectly right to test the character of these teachers by the doctrines they may teach. And especially so, since we are earnestly exhorted by one of beloved memory to do so, and who, in the affection of his heart, says, " Beloved, believe not every spirit, but try the spirits whether they are of God," 1 John iv : 1. An ancient writer says, " To the law and the testimony; if they speak not according to this word, it is because there is no light in them." Is. viii : 20. Taking, then, these principles for our guide, let us inquire what are the teachings of these spirits, who come commissioned from some quarter, to add, during the continuance of this dispensation, to the things which God hath authorized His servants to write in the book of His truth revealed to man. Rev. xxii : 18.

1. IN REFERENCE TO GOD.

Spiritualism teaches that there is a God who is Supreme and over all. Some individuals among them say, " There is no Supreme Spirit—each spirit is a God." " Thou believest that there is one God. Thou doest well: the demons also (*ta daimonia*) believe and tremble. But wilt thou know, O vain man, that faith without works is dead?"

The mere belief in the existence of a God is no proof of the goodness of the believer. All nations believe in some one Supreme Being, except the Parsees, the ancient Zoroasterites, who held to two first principles, one good, the other bad, which they look upon as two gods of equal power and from whom all things have sprung. The mythological system of India teaches that there is but one Being, from whom all the gods, and all things have sprung. In the worship of the many gods, they entirely overlook the worship of the One. Polytheism and Pantheism can be taught and believed, only where the light of Divine revelation does not shine.

But a question arises here—" What is God ? according to spirit teaching." Let them answer the question.

" You have said that the sun was pure fire, what do you think of it now?" was the question which was proposed by one to the spirit that purported to be the soul of one who had left the body, and had gone into the spirit-world, and was then speaking through the lips of a medium, a lady, the answer is—

"The sun which you behold is the God of heaven and earth."

"What do you mean by that?"

"Spirits know no other; and God has never been seen in any other form."

Some teach that "God is a spirit, and that the world is his body."

All this is, of course, blank, bald atheism.

What the particular views of God may be, which others of these spirits hold, or which spiritualists hold, we know not; but we have never yet read of one of these spirits teaching the Bible view of the character of God, nor do we know of a spiritualist that holds it. There is a uniform, invariable denial of the Scriptural representation of the Divine Being. The god they believe in is *not* the God that is revealed in the Bible.

2. WHAT THEY TEACH CONCERNING CHRIST.

The uniform teaching of all the spirits is, that Jesus is not Divine. Some call him the Son of God; but by that term they do not mean to express the idea of equality with the Father. He is the highest and the most exalted of creatures—he himself being a mere creature. According to the spirits, He did not die for the salvation of sinners; He did not make an atonement for sin; He did not come to destroy the works of the Devil; for they affirm there is no personal Devil. But as if to make certainty more sure, we have a published account of the conception, birth, and life of Jesus, which professes to be from Himself, and communicated through a medium a short time ago, in which

He flatly denies the account given of Him by the Evangelist Luke; He states he is nothing but a man, and never was anything more.

According to all this, the whole plan of salvation is a solemn farce. The preaching of faith and repentance, and the necessity of regeneration by the power of the Holy Spirit, (whose personal existence they deny,) and the sanctification of the soul as a prerequisite for the kingdom of God, are but a gilded lie. The wicked here of all grades, and those guilty of the basest of crimes, are not condemned, and never will be; but they pass immediately into a state of comparative happiness, where, by suffering, they make an atonement for their sins, and then begin to make progress in happiness and peace, and continue to increase in blessedness, and joy, and knowledge until they have attained the highest degree of glory, (in the ninth sphere according to some,) where they will forever be.

Expressions like the following, which purport to be communications from the spirits to their dearly beloved friends and former acquaintances in this city, are scattered in profuse abundance throughout the works that are published by Spiritualists:

"All are much happier in the spirit-world than they were on earth." "All are in a state of progression in the spirit-world; none remain where they enter; all will progress and enjoy as much happiness constantly as they are capable of receiving." "When the people begin to believe this *great truth*, the errors of the popular religion will then be abandoned." "Man can never be thoroughly reformed till God is divested of his artificial attributes." "So long as He is held up to man clothed in these false characters, man can never see Him in his true light; consequently, cannot appreciate Him in scarcely the smallest degree." The attribute of justice is particularly referred to here. " It [spiritualism] will bring about more good to mankind than any sectarian religion can possibly do."— " If you want to progress, you must let your mind dwell upon the beauties of nature and of the spirit home." (Not Christ and his salvation.) " This glorious destiny (future happiness) is prepared for all men without exception—none are to be excluded; all shall be happy." " None of the race of mankind is destined to be miserable. Unbounded happiness is prepared for all."

To a Baptist preacher from his sister in the spirit-world: "MY DEAR BROTHER:—You have been a believer in a dark and gloomy creed. There is no misery in any department of the spirit home, but progression is onward and upward! Our joy is unutterable. Man alone possesses the power of progression. He has progressed from the creation of the world, and is now much above his original condition on the earth. Now think of what we have said. We do not want you to harmonize it with the dark and gloomy popular religion. *This cannot be done.* Communications from us can never agree with *their* principal teachings. [True.] We believe in no God of anger and wrath. There is no such being. All is guided by infinite wisdom, love, and goodness."

These extracts give the spirit and marrow of this communication.

A son purports to write to his mother, and says : " My dear mother :—Pin not your faith on creeds and doctrines of faith. God is love. He loves all his intelligent creation, and this is sufficient to lead all who yield to its holy influence into the presence of the Great Creator."

Another: "MY DEAR GRANDCHILD :—The more we are talked to the better we can respond. It gives us more power to have you familiar with us." [No doubt it does.]

From a Son to his Mother. "MY DEAR MOTHER :— You have mourned for me; do so no more. Your loss has been my great gain. My happiness is much greater than you can conceive of. Spirits are all happy, and when you believe in spiritual manifestations, you will feel far happier than you now do. Then you will not fear the threats of hell and damnation that are preached to you. Such doctrine is wrong, and bad in its tendencies on the human mind, and has been the cause of much unbelief in the immortality of the soul, and infidelity to truth and righteousness."

From a Father to his Son. "MY DEAR SON :—You have much to learn. Your nature is progressive. We come to teach you this, and to aid you to develop your spiritual powers. We come to teach you that God is love; that the spirit of man is an *emanation* from Him, (Hindooism) and that man is a *unit!* that his *present social arrangements are wrong*, and opposed to his best interests in life, and in the one to come." (Would Socialism and Free-loveism be better?)

In a colloquy held with the spirits, the following questions were asked, to which the appended answers were given:

"Is the physical condition of man inferior to what it was formerly?

"No; it is more perfected.

"Does physical suffering retard spiritual development?

"No.

"Then man was not made originally as perfect, physically and spiritually, as he is now?

"No; many changes have taken place. He has progressed in his physical being with his spiritual development."

(See Spiritual manifestations in the city of Philadelphia, by a member of the First Circle. Pages 62-90. 1851.)

Thus the fall of man, his original righteousness and subsequent sinning, and all God's plans and purposes to redeem a fallen race, and save them through Jesus Christ, the only Redeemer, are perfectly ignored and set aside by these demoniacal revelations. True it is that their teachings can never harmonize with the Word of God, as revealed to us in the Bible.

3. THE TEACHINGS OF SPIRITS AS TO THE BIBLE.

On this subject there is a slight discrepancy among them, but the general idea is about the same. The extracts given already concerning the teachings of the spirits, show what are their general views as to the value of the Bible. But one of these spirits, professing to be the Apostle Paul, gives us his connected views on the whole Bible, which show certainly great progress in some direction. The spirit that took possession of the medium declared himself to be the Apostle. The question was asked this spirit,

"What think you of the Bible now, since your entrance into the spirit world?"

The answer was given in the following language:

Genesis—" About as true as any fictitious work now in print," p. 10.

Exodus—" As good a book as could have been expected at that day," p. 10.

Leviticus—" Not directly from God, as man supposes," p. 12.

Numbers—"Such an absurdity as that, [the facts stated in chap. 1st] ought to be cast into the lowest depth of the infernal regions," p. 13.

Joshua—" Almost the whole book is false," *Ib*.

Judges—" About the same as the others; and it needs no argument to show that it is void of inspiration," p. 14.

Ruth—" Without inspiration, the same as the others," p. 15.

Samuel—" A part of it is correct," p. 15.

Kings—" Multitudes of mistakes—not correct—no inspiration," pp. 16, 17.

Ezra—" By a person bearing its name, without inspiration," p. 17.

Job—" Written through mediums—would have been correct, had it not been that men destroyed its purity," pp. 18, 19.

Psalms—" Written in the same way and some of them correct," p 19.

The rest of the books of the Old Testament are said to be " somewhat correct in the main," p. 20.

" Let me say unto you, O man! at this day, in regard to the Old Testament, 'MENE, MENE, TEKEL, UPHARSIN,'" p. 21.

In passing through the Gospels, Epistles, and the Apocalipse, this vile spirit exclaims, " Not correct," " mistake," " fictitious," " contrary to the will of God." And to cap the whole, " Such, O man, are the principles the books you call the Bible, are conveying to the inhabitants of the earth. O horrible!" p. 92.

"The Old Testament, which Christ declared wrong and wicked, you are still calling the Word of God. ... Although your angelic fathers, by the wisdom of God, are allowed to come unto you, and do away with the wicked precepts of your Bible," pp. 93, 94.

Thus we have spirit testimony as to the value of the Sacred Scriptures. They make a clean sweep of it all.— And why should they not; for certainly the Scriptures condemn them most clearly. And with this rejection of the Bible, they reject also, all the doctrines which are the peculiarity and the glory of Christianity. "It is readily granted," says Mr. Brittan, "that spiritualism rejects the common notions respecting the fall of angels, total depravity, and the atonement." "We do also reject the resurrection as taught by accredited authorities in Mythological theology," and by this he means Christianity.

A mere glance at a few numbers of the "Spiritual Telegraph," or at any of the accredited works on spiritualism, is sufficient to convince any one that the teachings of spiritualism are the "teachings of Demons," or in our rendering of the passage, "doctrines of Devils," 1 Tim. iv: 1, and opposed to Christ and his salvation.

THE SPIRITS—WHO ARE THEY?

We have admitted the facts in the case, viz: that communications are really made by invisible, and by intelligent agents to the living at the present time. Who are they? Spiritualists, with one voice, say they are the spirits of good or bad men, who formerly lived on earth. They deny that there are any intelligent beings in the invisible world called 'angels,' who are a distinct class from the spirits of men. Is this so? We readily grant that we have no light on this subject except what we derive directly from the Bible. Does, then, the Bible teach that there is a distinct class of beings from the souls of men? If there be not, then the faith of the people of God, from the days of Adam down to the present time, has been misplaced, yea, more, all the world of men have been believing a falsity. That there are

ANGELS,

who are a distinct class of intelligent beings from men; whether in the body or out of it, is to our minds, most evident from the Scriptures. The word *Angellos* is Greek, and the word *Malak* is Hebrew, and both signify a *messenger*, an *angel*. These words are used both in the Old, and in the New Testament to mean (a) human messengers, or agents for others; 2 Sam. ii: 5. Mark i: 2. Jas. ii: 25; (b) officers of the churches, Hag. i; 13. Rev. i: 20; (c) Jesus Christ, Mal. iii: 1.; (d) created intelligences, both good and bad; Heb. i: 14. Jude 6. Now, because the word angel does, sometimes, mean a mere human being, it certainly is not good reasoning to say it can mean nothing else. The passage in Jude most clearly proves that there is a class of intelligent beings different from man. The apostle speaks of "the angels who kept not their *first estate*," (*ten archen*, their principality, as the marginal reading is.) This, most evidently conveys the idea that some of them *did* keep their first estate. Only those who kept *not* their first estate, but left their *own habitation* hath God reserved in everlasting chains under darkness, unto the judgment of the great day.

It is evident, then, from this passage that there must be a distinct class of beings, called angels, for these two obvious reasons, viz.:

(1.) All men have sinned, and have come short of the glory of God. Rom. iii: 23. There is no exception: they have *all* lost their first estate. Hence, men are a different class from those beings, only some of whom have lost their first estate, while others have kept theirs.

(2.) These angels are said to have left their *own* habitation. God cast those of them that sinned down to hell and delivered them into chains of darkness, to be reserved unto judgment. 2 Pet. ii: 4. They were cast down, and cast out of the place they formerly occupied. But, man was made on this earth. This earth was given to him at first—and although he has sinned, still he is here, and dwells upon it. He has not been cast out of it. This proves clearly that men and angels are different, and belong each to an order of beings peculiar to itself.

The Greek word *tartarosas* in 2 Pet. ii: 4, and rendered by "cast down to hell," or to cast into Tartarus, needs a word of explanation. The word Tartarus means, according to Greek writers, "in a physical sense, the bounds, or verge of this material system." So that God cast the rebel angels out of his presence, into that blackness of darkness where they will be forever deprived of the light of His countenance, and that place is, probably, at present, within the atmosphere of our earth. For we read that Satan is the Prince of the power of the air, as well as the Prince of this world.

In the book of Job, (chap. xxxviii: 4-7,) we read that when God laid the foundations of the earth, and the corner stone thereof, then the morning stars (*cocabai boker*) sang together: and all the sons of God (Benai Elohim) shouted for joy. By these terms intelligent beings most certainly are meant, and as they sang together, when the foundations of the earth were first laid, and as man was not made till the sixth day of the work of creation, after the world had been formed, it is manifest that there must be an order of beings, wholly distinct from Adam and Eve, for they were in existence, and sang this song of praise before our first parents were created.

There is but one more passage that we would adduce to prove that there are angels, a class of beings distinct from man, and that is in Heb. xii: 22–23. The apostle says, "Ye are come to Mount Zion, and unto the city of the living God, the heavenly Jerusalem, and to an *innumerable company of angels*, to the general assembly and church of the first born, which are written in heaven, and to God the Judge of all, and to *the spirits of just men* made perfect, and to Jesus the Mediator of the new covenant." Here we see that the apostle makes a distinction between *angels*, and the spirits of *just men*. He certainly does not consider them to be one and the same order of beings. If he did, why use such language?

Not to occupy more time on this part of the subject, it is evident that there is an order of beings wholly distinct from man, who are intelligent, and who have the power to communicate with each other and with other intelligent beings like man, if they are permitted to do so.

Taking this, then, as a fixed fact, we learn from the Bible that there are both good and bad angels; that they are numerous; that they are intelligent; that they are strong; and as wickedness does not, necessarily, diminish the strength of men or angels, wicked angels may have as much physical strength, after their fall, as they had before it. If good angels can communicate with men, and if they can move heavy stones (Matt. xxviii: 2,) and open prison doors, locking them up again (Acts xii: 7–19,) may not evil angels do the same things? We see no reason why they may not. We believe they do.

CHAPTER IV.

THE TRUTH.

Having, in all candor and truthfulness, so far as we know the truth in the case, given the view which the spiritualists hold on the subject of these manifestations, we now proceed to show that the whole thing, in its incipiency, progress, and aim, is the work of Satan.

If we can demonstrate the fact that these things cannot proceed from mere *disease;* nor from *good angels;* nor from the *spirits of good* or *bad men*, in or out of the body; then the conclusion is irresistible that *the whole work is of the Devil and his angels.* And this, by God's help, we will do.

These manifestations are not *diseases*, nor the mere effect of a peculiar *state of body or mind.*

The demoniacs, in the days of our Lord, were, in many cases, diseased; but these diseases were the effect of some derangement in the body, produced by some evil spirits, who attached themselves to them, or in some way unknown to us, dwelt in them. Our Lord spoke to the demon in the possessed, and not to the disease. The demon answered Him, and asked if He had come to torment him before the time. He asked permission, if cast out of the man, to go into the swine that "were a good way off feeding." The demon was cast out, and did go into the swine. This could not be a disease that could leave a man and seize upon swine a good way off. Nor was it the man himself who ran off and scared the swine; for, when the people came they saw the man sitting quietly and clad in proper garments, and in his right mind. To say that this was a mere disease, is absurdity itself run mad. And equally absurd is it to say that the manifestations now are mere diseases. The mediums of our day may be diseased; but their disease is the effect of spirit-power. We need not dwell on this point. See the history as recorded by Matt. viii: 28–34, and Mark v: 1–19. See also "Twells on Demoniacs."

THEY ARE NOT THE WORK OF GOOD ANGELS.

So far as we have any knowledge about the ministry of angels, we learn that they are *all* sent forth to minister for those or on account of those, who shall be (*tous mellontas*, about to become) the heirs of salvation. Heb. 1: 14. If this be the work of *all* of them, then it is evident that these spirits, which possess our modern demoniacs, or influence the mediums, are not good angels, for all of these angels are engaged in the good and blessed work of aiding and encouraging, and strengthening, and defending those who are, or are about to become the heirs of salvation; whereas these spirits, in our day, are engaged in a very different kind of work. They are engaged in afflicting God's people; in turning away the people from hearing the truth; in leading them to deny the Bible, and all the great doctrines which flow out from that grand central truth, God manifest in the flesh. Good angels cannot engage in a bad work. It is evident from this single view of the subject that these varied manifestations cannot proceed from good angels.

There are now left us but two sources, for which these manifestations can possibly come, viz., either from the spirits of departed human beings, or from Satan and his hosts of evil spirits. The first of these is the one held by spiritualists to be the true one.

THEY ARE NOT SPIRITS OF THE DEAD.

Are these spirit manifestations produced by the spirits of departed human beings; and do the communications which are made, come from human beings in the invisible world, as they purport to be?

This is what spiritualists affirm, and in this faith we doubt not, many, probably nearly all, fully confide. Some there are, who say they know not what to think of them. We do not call in question the sincerity of any one of the multitudes who really think that they do at times converse with their departed friends. There is something very comforting to the sorrowing heart to be assured that the departed one is happy. We wish all our departed friends to be so. We hope they are; but to know that fact, if it could be known, would relieve the mourning friends of half their grief, wipe away their tears, and turn their mourning into gladness. This, spiritualism professes to do. And it is this, which renders the deception so fascinating, and so comforting too, in this aspect of the subject, that it is difficult, and in many cases will be impossible to break the enchantment. God alone can do that.

We might demand of the spiritualists the proof that the spirit of some departed one does come and communicate with them through the medium. Why cannot these departed ones communicate with their former friends in the flesh directly, without the intervention of a table or a third person? There is some difficulty in the case; and it is answered, the conditions are not favorable; but, hereafter, when the world of human beings, in the flesh, shall have developed their moral and physical nature, under the teachings of spirits, then the intercourse between the visible and the invisible worlds will again be renewed and established on a firm and unchanging basis forever. This will be the millennial age of the world. But such positive proof, convincing and assuring they cannot give, that can satisfy the enquiring soul. Even on their own minds there is a doubt left—for granting, as they do, that there are evil spirits, and lying spirits, they may be deceived by them, and they cannot be certain that they are not. We apprehend that none of the firmest believers in these spiritual communications would be willing to surrender up their personal property to some of their neighbors, who could bring forward no better, no stronger proof that the property in question belonged to them, than these spiritualists do that these communications are veritable communications from their departed friends. Why then should they trust their salvation on so slight a foundation?

But while we might demand the proof that these spirits *are* the spirits of the departed from earth, we affirm that they cannot be such.

For (1) if the spirits of the good are in heaven with God and Christ, then certainly they are not roaming all over the earth, disquieted by every Witch of Endor, and forced to appear at the summons of any spiritualist who may attempt to evoke them from their rest.

But (2) if the dead are in an intermediate place of partial blessedness or misery, then certainly they cannot be traversing this earth and communicating with mankind.—Neither the rich man nor Lazarus could communicate with surviving friends.

Or (3) if, as some teach, the dead are in a state of profound slumber till the resurrection, then their intercourse with mankind is a manifest impossibility.

Without stopping to discuss these respective theories, we simply remark that upon either of them the theory of spiritual manifestations is untrue.

That a few of the saints have appeared on earth after their departure from it, is what the Scriptures teach.—Elijah was taken up to heaven, B. C. 896. Moses died B. C. 1451—that is, some 555 years before the translation of Elijah. Both of these persons appeared on the mount of transfiguration with our Lord.—Matt. xvii: 1-4. Some suppose that this was a mere vision (Matt. xvi: 9) of the bodies of Moses and Elijah, and that they were not in reality present. But we think, with Calvin and others, that they were really present.

Quite a number of the bodies of the saints which slept came out of their graves, after the resurrection of our Lord, and went into the Holy City, and appeared unto many.—Matt. xxvii: 52, 53. We have no account of anything that they did beyond their mere appearance; and we have no authority to say that they did do or say anything to any of the living.

In Rev. xxii: 9.—The angel (*angelos*, messenger) who had been sent to John to communicate to him the book of Revelation, states distinctly that he was his "fellow servant, and of his brethren, the prophets, and of those who keep the sayings of this Book." He forbade John to pay him religious reverence, but bade him worship God. In this case there was no possession; the messenger appeared in his own person. And so it was with all the others of whom we read in the Scriptures. None of them ever appeared except in his own person and in *his own body.*

But since the day that revelation was closed for *this dispensation,* we have no account of any of the saints of the Lord that have ever returned to earth. Nor does God design that they should. Revelation is filled up until the Lord shall come again. Under that new state of the church and of the world, there will be, doubtless, new communications of God's will to man adapted to that peculiar state. But at present the Gentile church has, in the New Testament, all the knowledge that God means to impart to her. Communications from any one from the spirit-world informing us of our duty, would be, in fact, to set aside the teachings of the Bible which God has already given us.— If men will not hear Moses and the prophets, and also the words of Christ and of his apostles, neither would they hear, though one could come from the dead. The time is coming, however, and it may be very nigh at hand, when the prediction of our Lord in John 1 : 51—"Hereafter ye shall see the angels of God ascending and descending to (*epi,* Matt. xxiv : 16) the Son of man"—shall be literally fulfilled. And then will be fulfilled that part of the 72d Psalm, which is so often sung in our churches and so little believed,

"Angels descend with songs again,
And Earth repeat the loved Amen."

OPINIONS OF THE HEATHEN.

It is doubtless true that some of the ancient Greek and Roman philosophers and wise men of antiquity did hold that the demons were the souls of departed human beings, and that they did really take at times possession of the bodies of the living, and were the guardians of the people. Some of them were good, and some became bad.

Hesiod, the celebrated Greek poet who lived b. c. 900, tells us, in his "Works and Days," that " In the golden-age, when Saturn reigned in heaven, men lived like gods, free from evils, and died just as if they had fallen asleep; they became demons by the will of Jupiter, the great, powerful, dwelling upon the earth—guards of mortal men. They observe the good and evil done here; they are clothed with air, (invisible,) and roam over the earth everywhere; they are innumerable, the immortal guards of mortal men."—*Op. Hesiod, Lib.* 1.

According to this idea, the souls of men, after their departure from this world, become the inspectors of human affairs, and as they dispensed good to mankind, they were called demons. But others make them also "the dispensers of evil things as well as good to mankind, the plagues and the terrors of man, and the authors of much evil to them."—*Proclus in Hesiod.* See also *Euseb. Præp. Ev., Lib.* 3. *c.* 3.

Homer, the cotemporary of Hesiod, makes Minerva "retire to heaven to the palace of Jupiter and the other demons, *meta daimonas allous.*" These demons were "such as are removed from this life."—See *Iliad i : v.* 222. *Proclus in loco.*

But this is not the opinion held by others of the heathen philosophers.

Thales, the famous Greek philosopher, who died b. c. 548, held that the demons are spiritual beings, who never had been embodied as men. He divides the deities into three calsses, viz.: *Theos*—God, the mind of the world, *Psuchikai*—Demons, spiritual beings; and the Heroes, *Heroes*. The Heroes are the souls of departed men—of these the good are divine (*agathas*); the bad are vile (*phaulas*.)

PLATO, who died B. C. 348, says (in *Sympsio*): "*Pan to Daimonion metaxu esti Theou te kai thnetou.*—The demons hold a middle place between God and men."

Clemens Alexandrinus, in speaking of Plato, says: "*HO Platon de kai tois theois,*" &c. Plato attributes a peculiar dialect to the gods, inferring this from dreams and oracles, and from the demoniacs, who do not speak their own language or dialect, but that of the demons who were entered into them.—*Clem. Alex. Strom. i.*

APULIUS, A. D. 40, (*de Dæmonio Socratis*) says of these demons, "They are immortal, without beginning or end, always existing from eternity.—*Immortales, sine ullo vel fine vel exordio, sed prorsus a retro æviterni.*"—Vid. Mede, p. 627. They certainly then could not be human spirits.

PLUTARCH, who died about A. D. 140, makes two classes of demons, viz.: (1) Souls separate from bodies, and (2) such as never dwelt in bodies at all. Both are called demons.—See *Plut. de defect. Orac.*

LUCIAN, who died about A. D. 181, speaks of some in his day who "delivered the demoniacs from their terrors."— He then alludes to our Lord, as that Syrian of Palestine who cured the sick man, saying, "The man is silent, but the demon (*ho daimon*) answers either in the language of the Greeks or Barbarians, or whatsoever country he be. But he exorcising the demon, and also threatening him, if he did not obey, drives out the demon, *exelaunei ton dai-*

mona." Lucian was no Christian, and hence his testimony is not without value.—Lucian in Philopsend, p. 833.

It is said by some that the Jews held, in common with some of the heathen, that the demons were the spirits of men, and that Josephus is of this number. True; he says in his work, (De Bello Jud. Lib. 7. c. 23,) "*Daimonia tauta poneron estin anthropon pneumata*"—which may be rendered, "These demons are the spirits of evil men."— This seems to be the correct translation of the words; but whether he held that they were the spirits of bad men having entered into the bodies of others, or that these demons are spirits possessing evil men, we shall not decide. The former idea would be contrary to his faith as a Pharisee, and to the teachings of the Old Testament; and yet he might have believed it. (See Twills on Demoniacs.)

FAITH OF THE PRIMITIVE CHRISTIANS.

It is a matter of very little consequence what the heathen of antiquity believed on the subject of demoniacs. We see they were divided in their opinion. But we think the heathen world at the present time would give a united testimony in favor of the demoniacs being evil angels, as distinct from the spirits of departed men.

That the Christians of the first and second centuries believed in the reality of demoniacal possessions, cannot be doubted by any one who has read the early history of the church. They had power also to cast these evil spirits out of the possessed. The number of those who were afflicted by these evil spirits, and who had been relieved, was great. Many of them were converted and were received into the church. They formed a distinct class of Christians, and were under the special care and direction of the exorcists in the Primitive Church, and for a while were kept separate from the others. When they became perfectly restored from the diseases produced by the possession, they were permitted to unite with the congregation in public worship, and to partake of the Lord's Supper.— Some of these believers were at times afflicted by these evil spirits, as well as those who were not Christians; and in all cases these demons were subject to the authority and name of Jesus Christ. (See Dr. Coleman's Primitive Christianity.

We hesitate not to express our firm belief that the demons spoken of in the New Testament were fallen angels, under the control and guidance of Satan; and that the spiritual manifestations which are witnessed in this country, and in various portions of the Christian world, are in like manner the work of the same evil angels. This was the belief of the church in the first and second centuries, as to the demoniacal possessions then. Of this fact there is an abundance of proof.

JUSTIN MARTYR, a Christian Father, who died A. D. 165, in his dialogue with Trypho the Jew, says that "the gods of the heathen are demons, *Daimones eisi oi Theoi ton ethnon.*" This is the Greek translation of Ps. xcvi. 5, which in our translation reads "all the gods of the nations are idols (*elilim* vanities.") In speaking of Satan's deceiving our first parents, he calls him the "man-hating demon.—*Ho misanthropos Daimon.*" It would seem from this use of the word, that he held these demons to be evil spirits, a distinct class of beings from the souls of departed men.

In his apology to the enemies of Christianity, Justin says, "many Christians throughout the world, and even in your own city, simply by calling upon the name of Jesus Christ, have healed many that were possessed of evil spirits, and still continue to heal such."

IRENÆUS, a little later in the second century, says, "that many through grace, received, from the Son of God who was crucified under Pontius Pilate, power to heal the sick, to cast out demons, and raise the dead; that multitudes throughout the world daily exercised these gifts, without any magic, charm, or secret art, but merely by calling on the name of our Lord Jesus Christ." *Adv. Hær.* ii, 57.

TATIAN, a Christian writer of the same age, A. D. 170, says expressly, that "the demons who govern man are not the souls of men, *ouk Eisin oi ton anthropon psuchai.*"— Orat. cont. Græcos, p. 154. On a previous page he says (p. 148,) of demons, that "they were ejected from the heavenly life, *ekbletoi tes en ourano diaites gegenemenoi,*" that is, they were fallen angels.

THEOPHILUS ANTIOCHENUS, who was cotemporary with Tatian, says, (Lib.2, ad autocl., p. 1, 4,) that he who tempted Eve in Paradise, was "that mischievous demon called Satan, *ho kakopoios Daimon, ho kai Satan kaloumenos.*" He could not possibly hold that this demon was the spirit of a dead man of the human race, when as yet there were none who had died.

TERTULLIAN, of Carthage, who lived at the close of the second century, appeals to Scapula, the Roman Governor of that province, and tells him that he had officers under him who were indebted to Christians for acts of kindness, though they might now oppose them, and then adds, "for the Secretary himself is one who has been delivered from an evil spirit." "One may thank a Christian for the healing of a relative, another for that of a son." *Ter. ad Scapulam.*

Tertullian held that these "demons were invisible beings, endowed with spiritual power, living in the air, attending constantly on particular persons. They inflict on men's bodies diseases, and various grievous afflictions. They are the occasion of men going suddenly and extraordinarily mad. The subtlety and fineness of their nature enables them to enter into the bodies and the souls of men. Being spirits, they have great power. They can act though they are invisible, and incapable of being felt; and you must judge by the effect upon men, rather than by their act, which is invisible."

Tertullian does not maintain that these demons are the spirits of departed men; for he says, "*esse substantias quasdam spiritales, &c.*" "that they are certain spiritual substances," while he defines the human soul to be "*corporalis,*" material. He also makes the demons to be authors of the fall of man. *Apol. adv. Gent. c. xxii. De Anima c. xi: xxii.*

CYPRIAN, A. D. 250, held that the demons were fallen angels, the evil spirits who inspired the breasts of the heathen prophets, who are the authors of oracles, who creep into men's bodies, destroy their health, and cause diseases." *Cyp. de Idolat.*

ARNOBIUS, A. D. 300, says that "the name of Jesus once heard, puts the evil spirits to flight, silences the prophets, and makes the diviners foolish." *Arnob. adv. Gent.* Lib. 1, § 46, p. 74.

LACTANTIUS, A. D. 310, following his preceptor, Arnobius, says, "Let there be set before us one who, it is certain, is possessed by a demon, and the Delphic priest or prophet; we shall see them both in the same manner terrified at the name of God, and Apollo will with the same haste depart out of his prophet, as the spirit will out of the demoniac." Lib. iv. c. xxvii, 13, 14. "These demons being adjured by the name of the true God, immediately depart," p. 321, ed. 1698.

EUSEBIUS says that "the Heathen Prophecies and Oracles proceed from *evil spirits*," and by this he means fallen angels.—*Lib. v. c.* 4.

DEMONS ARE SUBJECT TO CHRIST'S NAME.

In the "Martyrdom of Ignatius," sec. 4, Ignatius addresses the Emperor Trajan, saying, "But, if because I am a trouble to those evil spirits, you call me wicked, I confess the charge; for having within me Christ, the Heavenly King, I dissolve all the snares of those demons." *Wake's Epis. Apos. Fathers*, p. 131.

THEOPHILUS of Antioch, says, "Demoniacs are sometimes, even to this day, exorcised in the name of the living God, and these deceitful spirits confess themselves to be demons, *kai omologei auta ta plana pneumata einai Daimones*."—*Ad. Autocl. Ed. Ox. l.* 2, *p.* 77.

IRENÆUS, speaking of the miraculous powers given to the true disciples of Christ, says, that they dispossessed evil spirits, exorcising them in the name of Christ. "Some," he says, "certainly and truly eject demons, *oi men gar daimones elaunousi bebaios kai alethōs*." He speaks of "others who heal the sick by the imposition of hands, and restore them whole, *alloi de tous*," &c.—*Adv. Hær. l.* 2, *c.* 57.

ORIGEN says, so great was the power of the name of Jesus against demons that it has success, even when named by wicked persons, as Jesus himself taught in Matt. vii: 22, " Many will say, in that day, have we not cast out devils, (*Demons*) in thy name—then will I profess unto them, I never knew you." " It is plain that Christians use none of the arts of enchanters, but the name of Jesus Christ."— *Orig. Cont. Cels., l.* 1.

The case of the seven sons of Sceva, the Jew, (Acts xix: 13-20,) is a proof of the fact that wicked men have tried to cast out demons, by using the name of Jesus. And when our Lord was charged by the Jews, for casting out demons, as being in league with the devil, He asks them by what authority their children cast out evil spirits. He does not deny the fact that they did do so. Matt. xii: 22-30.

Cyprian, in writing to Demetrianus, the Proconsul of Africa, a bitter enemy of Christians, says, " O! that you would see and hear the gods of the Gentiles, when they are adjured by us and tormented by our spiritual scourges; and cast out of the bodies they possessed, by the force of our words, when crying out, and lamenting with a human voice, and feeling the strokes of a Divine power, they confess the judgment to come: *O si audire eos, Deos Gentium, velles et videre,*" &c.—*Cypr. Op. Ed. Ox., p.* 191.

Lactantius says that " the spirits adjured by the name of God depart out of bodies." As Christ himself cast out all demons by his word, so do his followers now cast the same impure spirits out of men, both in the name of their Master, and by the sign of His passion." *Lactan. de Sapient., l.* 4, *c.* 27.

These quotations are quite sufficient to show us what the general opinion of the Christian Church, in the first centuries of the Christian era was, in reference to these demons. They doubtless maintained that they were really and truly some of the fallen angels, who are under the control of Satan, the Prince of the power of the air. The idea that they are the souls of departed human beings is without sufficient foundation, though the theory has now many advocates.

But if we take into consideration the simple facts in the case, we must be convinced that the possessions in the days of our Lord, were by evil angels or spirits, wholly distinct from disease or from the souls of men. The facts are such as these, viz:

1. They knew our Lord. Mark i: 24.
2. They spoke to him, and made requests of him. Mark v: 7.
3. The possessed were not always diseased, but sometimes merely dumb or blind. Matt. ix: 32.
4. Our Lord makes a distinction between healing diseases and casting out demons. Mark i: 34.
5. The demoniacs themselves say that they were possessed by evil spirits. The Jews said the same thing, and so did the apostles. And our Lord says he cast them out. Matt. iv: 25; Luke xi: 19.
6. When the seventy disciples returned from one of their tours in preaching, one part of their joy was that the demons were subject to their authority when they used the name of Christ Jesus. Our Lord told them he saw Satan as lightning fall from heaven; and bade them not rejoice so much, that *the spirits* were subject to them as that their names were written in heaven. Luke x: 18.
7. These demons had a degree of knowledge and of power, which no human being ever had on earth. They

knew that it was not the time fixed for their punishment when our Lord was on the earth. Such a knowledge was never revealed to man while on the earth, and no one can prove that the spirit of a man, after his departure from this world, receives such knowledge of the future. The strength of the demoniac was supernatural for man, and if we do not allow he was assisted by an evil spirit, it will be impossible to account for his wonderful strength.

8. The Bible speaks of the Devil and his angels. Matt. xxv: 41; and if these which possess men are not his angels, it will be impossible to find them. Our Lord, we are told, went about doing good, and healing all who were oppressed by the Devil. Now it is not likely that Satan should not employ his angels to oppress men in the flesh, but should employ the spirits of departed men to do that work for him, while his own angels are unemployed and idle.

9. Unless we suppose the demons to be of the number of those who were cast out of heaven, it will be difficult to understand our Lord's remark, in Luke x: 18, where He says he saw Satan like lightning fall from heaven, when taken in connection with the saying of the seventy, that the demons were subject to them through His name. Our Lord and they referred to the same beings.

It appears to us impossible to give any other explanation of these demons of the New Testament, that will solve all the difficulties in the case, unless we allow that they are really and truly evil angels, under the control of Satan, their prince and ruler. With this view, everything concerning them is plain; without it the whole history is obscured and involved.

SPIRITS NOW SUBJECT TO CHRIST.

If now we look at the present manifestations, and compare them with the demonical possessions of the Scriptures, no one can fail to perceive their striking similarity; and we think must see that they are works more in accordance with the workings of Satan and evil angels, than with the works of good spirits or of the holy saints or angels.

It is evident that the effects produced upon the bodies of men, women and children in this country and in heathen lands, at the present time, are similar to those that were produced in the times of our Lord. And what is equally striking in the case, is that all of them are subject to the name of Jesus. Command any wicked sinner here, or in India, for example, in the name of Christ to be silent, and what will the effect be? Probably he will curse you to your face, and will repeat that holy name with scorn. But, speak to a person possessed in any circle of spiritualists now, and command the spirit in the medium, the possessed one, in the name of Jesus of Nazareth to be silent, to depart from the person, or to leave the house altogether, and the effect upon the spirit is the same now that it was then. Evil spirits are compelled to submit to the authority of Jesus. They do it. But men in the flesh do not.

There are instances in abundance on record, where these evil spirits have given responses to the inquiries, and when they have been adjured in the name of Christ to tell the truth, they have confessed themselves to be liars, and that their sole object was to deceive mankind. We might suppose that, after such a manifest proof of their satanic mission, the spiritualists would see the impropriety, and the folly of seeking information from such a lying source. But no; the delusion is strong: and the very fact that the questioner has compelled the spirit to answer correctly, gratifies him, and still leads him on to ask from this lying spirit other questions to which he will give again lying answers, or such as might gratify the pride or vanity of the enquirer. Thus step by step the person is led along, until, having become accustomed to hear the truth of God's word called in question, or perverted, he insensibly begins to think that the Bible may be false in some things, or if not, that it should receive another interpretation which just as effectually destroys its power over him as if it were false. The man that begins to doubt the truth of God's word is already ensnared by the Devil. He may escape; but he should cry to God for help.

We have already said that men do not lose their physical powers now by their increase in wickedness: nor did the angels lose their power by becoming wicked. The devil contended with Michael the arch-angel about the body of Moses, (Jude 9) which shows us that he retains his strength still. He carried the body of our Lord up through the air, and placed it on the pinnacle of the temple. (See Matt. iv: and Luke iv.) The spirits broke the fetters, and chains of the demoniac, and no power of man could forge bands and chains too strong for the evil spirits to break. Good angels opened barred doors, and rolled away the huge stone that was at the door of the sepulchre of our Lord; and Philip was carried through the air by the spirit of the Lord and was set down at Azotus. We have no right to suppose that the evil angels are not as strong now as they were before their fall, and that they do not equal the good angels in strength. From all we can learn from the Bible and from all we see of their operations now, we judge it is the case.

THESE SPIRITS ARE THE EMISSARIES OF SATAN.

This is their true character. We are forced into this belief from considerations such as the following:

1. They do at times recall facts that are past ages ago, which no living man could know, but which are found afterwards to be true, or at least so probable that they cannot well be doubted.

2. They do unsettle the minds of many, and do lead many into madness, insanity and ruin.

3. They have never yet been known to reveal any truth important for man to know, that is not already revealed to us in the Word of God, or that has not been discovered by the scientific aid of good men.

4. They have never yet been known to lead one sinner to Jesus Christ for the pardon of his sins, and for the sanctification of his soul, nor is there one of the two millions of spiritualists now in the land that has been savingly converted to God by spiritualism. They may have rapped the Universalism of one man, and the Atheism of another, out of them, and have made them believe that there is a God, and a future state; but this is no more, after all, than the faith of the devil himself; and how much better are such believers in reference to future bliss, than they were before, or than Satan himself? Not a particle. Now, with all this ado about progress, and the New Philosophy, what, we ask, is the benefit of these manifestations that never yet did, and never can result in the pardon of one sin, or in the sanctification of one soul?

5. These spirits most carefully, studiously, invariably at all times, in all places, and under all circumstances, give their testimony against the Word of God, and the plan of salvation that therein is made known to sinful man. Their invariable feeling towards Jesus is the same that it ever has been. "Jesus of Nazareth, let us alone; what have we to do with thee?" (Mark v: 24.) And what fellowship hath light with darkness, or Jesus with evil spirits?

They deny the fall of man; they deny the fact of Christ's atonement, and its necessity for the salvation of man, and by one fell stroke, sweep away the whole plan and purpose of God as revealed through the Mediator between God and man, the man Christ Jesus. This is the invariable teaching of the spirits. And if there be a spiritualist who yet holds a different view of the subject, it is because he had been previously taught so, for spiritualism does not teach the necessity of salvation through the atoning blood of Christ. And if Christ and his salvation be taken away the remainder will be of no saving benefit to the soul.

AN OBJECTION ANSWERED.

It is said that spiritualism must be good, and from God, because many sick have been healed by or through the agency of mediums; and it is triumphantly asked, would Satan do a good thing?

We reply, that for ourselves, we have no doubt that Satan has a more thorough knowledge of the nature of the soul and body of man, than the most profound metaphysician, and the most learned anatomist in the world; yea, that he knows more than all of them together. He has been a stupid scholar if he does not. A course of study for six thousand years, by a mind that forgets nothing, and by one who can look into the mysteries of nature, must bring in results which must infinitely (we might almost say,) surpass all that a fallen man of threescore years and ten can possibly attain. But wisdom is not goodness; and doing a good act from a bad motive, is not good in itself, though it may be a good to some individual. The fisherman will bait his hook well; but it is to deceive and catch the silly fish. And why should not Satan, who must certainly know, in many cases, what will heal diseases, prescribe the remedy, when he knows that by so doing he will gain the confidence of the restored one in the skill of the medium, and thus get honor to himself, who prescribes in the case. Surely Satan would have no objections to heal all the infirmities that "flesh is heir to," if he could, by so doing, lead men to forsake the law of the Lord, and not to place their faith and hope in Christ. The few good things that may be done through the instrumentality of mediums, who may be sincere in all they do, can never compensate for the evils that must follow in the wake of these operations.

It is also said that many men, since they have embraced spiritualism, have become better men, so far as temper and disposition, and treatment of their families are concerned. We are always glad to hear that men have become moral, even if they do not become godly. But still, we say that while this change has taken place, it has been produced by such an agency, as to make them, if possible, more opposed to the plan of salvation through our Lord Jesus Christ, than they were before. Where, then, is the ultimate gain to them? We ask the questions, and let the two millions of spiritualists in this country answer them. Does spiritualism teach its followers to love and reverence the Word of God, the Bible, more? Does it lead them to love the Church of Christ more? Does it lead them to send out missionaries to the heathen, and to tell them of a Redeemer for lost man? Does it lead them to believe on the Lord Jesus Christ alone for salvation from sin here, and for glory hereafter? The answer, we hesitate not to say, will be to each and all of these questions, a decided no. Can such a faith be from God? or can the agencies which lead to such results, be from God? Surely they cannot be.

THERE IS WISDOM HERE.

We are well aware that many good people, and many worthy ministers of Christ, are disposed to treat this whole subject with what might be called sovereign contempt.— They think, or at least they say, that such things as table-turning, table-tipping, and rappings, noises, writing music, &c., are so supremely ridiculous, so far beneath the dignity of any mind, that even Satan himself would not condescend to trouble himself with them. They have a higher opinion of Satan than that. It is too great a stoop for his angelic mind. Hence they affirm that the whole thing is a *trick;* and because some do make money by it, they affirm that all are alike, all are cheats or deceivers, and are palming off upon the people for realities, what they know to be falsities and lies. Such words of emptiness prove nothing. They rather confirm the unhappy subject of these operations in their defence of them, than show them how they may escape out of the fowler's snare.

But so far from these things being supremely ridiculous and the manifestations of folly, there is in them a depth of cunning, and a profoundness of wisdom, and a far-reaching plan, which it falls not to the wisdom of man to devise. If it be the object of the Evil One to deceive and mislead man, and if it be his interest to conceal his own agency, and to urge on his victim to acts and thoughts increasingly hostile to God, by means seemingly consistent with, and apparently proceeding from man's natural powers, we can easily understand why phenomena—trivial in themselves, but admirably adapted to excite curiosity and open up fresh grounds for research—should be selected, and how facts of a more prominent and imposing description would have been utterly unsuitable for such a purpose.

Every one knows that slight interferences with the ordinary course of events are far more thrilling and exciting than larger manifestations of power. Go into your bedchamber, for example, and lie down upon your bed, in the stillness and the quiet of the night, and a slight rustling of the bed-curtains; a gentle pulling at the bed-cover; the real or imaginary foot-fall of some one on the floor; a slight tapping noise; or a mistaken moaning of the wind, will produce more mental disturbance and more anxiety of mind, and will rob you of more hours of sleep, than the vivid lightning-flash or the heavy crash of God's voice of thunder in the heavens.

It is precisely so with these spirit-manifestations of which we are speaking. People may laugh at them, and ministers of Christ may speak contemptuously of them; but Satan knows what he is doing. He has not devised this plan for naught; and never did he broach a more cunning and plausible scheme to ruin souls in an enlightened land than this. It would not do for a heathen world, but here it will; for it tends in an especial manner to foster the pride of the unsanctified heart, by extolling reason and placing it above the inspiration of the Word of God. This plan falls in with the godless intellectualism of the age. Science, in the hands of these men, arrays herself against revelation. They vainly suppose that the chapters which God has written on the stars in the heavens, on the hidden and visible rocks of the earth, and on earth's rugged and scarred face, must of necessity contradict what He hath written by the pen of Moses in the book of the creation. Surely God cannot contradict, in the work of his hands, what He has written in the book of Revelation. What astronomer or geologist, who is not deceived through the pride of his heart, can suppose that God, who is the Author of nature and of Revelation, can in the least degree contradict his own testimony, wherever and however it may be given?— And yet Satan would make men believe that, by reason and by science, they have made the discovery that God's Word, as revealed in the Bible, does not mean what it says.

We would put down naught in malice on this subject, but would seek to speak the truth in love, and seek to show just what this last device of Satan does set forth to man in place of God's own unchanging truth.

"The grand aim and tendency of Spiritualism," says a medium of high authority, "is to unite mankind in harmony." Hence spirit intercourse operates—

"1. Negatively, by removing obstacles to practical reform arising from undue concentration of mind on *future interests*, to neglect of present duties. People are so intent on saving themselves from a supposed external and distant danger, that they ruin themselves internally by neglecting the culture of their higher and inner nature. Expecting to be *saved by something external*, they become selfish and degraded, so as to be incapable of realizing anything but a low phase of being, here or elsewhere. A belief in spiritual intercourse stimulates to self-culture and social reform."

" 2. *Positively*, by spreading a knowledge of the laws of life and health, physical and spiritual; by energizing principles of love and wisdom, causing a desire for a true physical and a higher form of social life, measurably free from the *selfish element*, gratifying the social faculties by association with congenial minds; by developing our own spiritual nature, so that we can more readily perceive *affinities, matrimonial* and otherwise. Those in communion with a class of spirits above them, run no risk of forming uncongenial matrimonial relations, as a spirit out of the form can perceive affinities more readily than a person in the natural body; consequently, marriages formed by them will be happy ones, and the offspring of such, gentle and loving, harmonizing the future."—*Epitome of Spirit Intercourse*, p. 95.

In plain English, we are here taught (1) that a fixedness of mind upon the great interests of the soul and of our future eternal interests, is an obstacle to practical social reform in society; or, in other words, the best reformers of society are those who think least about the interests of the soul, and who are not like one who said, "My heart is fixed, trusting in the Lord."

(2.) That our salvation and future life depend upon the culture and development of our inner nature, and a knowledge of the laws of life, and not upon Christ, who is our life.

(3.) That the higher form of social life is that freedom

from the "selfish element" which says, "let every man have his *own* wife, and let every woman have her *own* husband. Let the husband render unto the wife due benevolence, and likewise also the wife unto the husband."—1 Cor. vii : 2, 3. The Free Love system is the *beau ideal* of social bliss.

(4.) That Christianity which teaches that the soul of man is saved by something external, or out of himself, viz.: by the blood and atonement of Christ, degrades human nature, and makes it selfish.

Here, then, we have the sum and substance of this boasted life, this new philosophy, this great scheme of social reform and of human regeneration, to which all these spirit manifestations would lead us. Such a system of doctrines as this, that excludes Christ and his salvation; that denies his Divine nature, and debases him to the level of a mere creature; that denies the redemption of the soul by the meritorious death of Christ; that rejects the Bible, the Word of God, as being a true revelation from God, and the only infallible rule of faith and practice, and with it all the doctrines it contains, is one of the devices of the Devil, by which he will receive for himself a temporary power, such as he has not yet had, over the souls of men, before his final ejection from this world by the brightness of the coming of the Son of man.

The few acts of relief to suffering humanity that may be performed by the so-called healing mediums, through spirit agency, supposing them all to be veritable realities, are but a part of the grand system of Satanic deception, by which the multitudes are led to place more confidence in them and less in God. It is the lure in the great game of life by which mortals, having gained a temporary respite from bodily pain, are emboldened to trust their soul's salvation in the hands of this skillful player, and lose their all, soul and body, at a throw. Oh! it is a sad sight to see rational beings calmly and deliberately stepping from off the Rock of Ages, and venturing their eternal hopes upon the quicksands of Satanic fraud! Probation ended here, they are eternally undone unless they be found in Christ. But this Arch-deceiver would cheat poor, deceived humanity, by assuring them that man's destiny is one of final, endless bliss; that progress, and progress in and toward perfect fellowship with God, is the law of our nature, and which must so develop itself, without a Saviour and without an atonement for the sins of man.

Let us not be ignorant of Satan's devices. No earthly reform of human device can save this world from the righteous judgments of an insulted and offended God. This earth is destined for a baptism of fire. God has so declared it. And although Satan, who is neither omniscient nor omnipresent, holds now a permitted yet restricted usurpation of this world, and exercises his implacable opposition to God and man, yet he cannot surpass the limits which Jehovah, our God, has prescribed for him. God's pre-determined plans and purposes are moving onward, steadily and rapidly, and will infallibly result in the re-establishment of his authority and his will throughout the length and breadth of this wide creation. Satan, powerless to arrest the purposes of God, is ever watching his opportunity to oppose and disturb them, and is adapting his operations to veil and to resist the new developments of God's purposes as they successively appear. His vast intellectual resources; his practical knowledge of the human heart; his uninterrupted acquaintance with the entire history of this world for the past 6000 years combined with his unquestionable knowledge of the probable future, so far as he is able to obtain it by the exercise of a profound intelligence in the examination of the records of revealed truth, not omitting his access to heavenly places, and the incalculable number of his subordinate agents, all combine to impress us with the immensity of his sway, and with the greatness of that warfare which is going on between him and the Son of God.

The deep and unfathomable mystery of those events predicted in the Word of God; of Satan's opposition to holiness and to God; of his binding for a thousand years in the abyss, and of his subsequent release for a season; and of his final and eternal banishment from God—his being cast into the lake of fire, with all those who may have been deceived by him, should be no barrier to their reception and belief. They are clearly written for our instruction. And whether men believe what God has revealed to us or not, He will none the less certainly do His work, His strange work, and bring to pass His act, His strange act upon the earth. Is. xxvii: 21.

WHY THESE MANIFESTATIONS NOW?

Satan always has a reason for what he does, and we may be assured that there can be no special manifestation of Satanic power or device, unless it be to oppose some special plan or purpose of God with which he may have been made acquainted, or which on the eve of being developed, he would, if possible, resist. The plans of God have all been laid back in the ages of eternity. They are all gradually being developed, and fulfilled. To us these plans cannot be known, except as they may be revealed to us in the

Word of God, or in their actual accomplishment. And even those that are revealed to us, most clearly in the Word of God, are concealed from us, in many cases, by the devices of Satan. He often forces men to put a wrong interpretation upon the promises and the predictions of the Word of God, so that we may be kept in ignorance of their true import. By so doing we lose the encouragement the promise is designed to give us: and we neglect to prepare for the events which the prediction assures are coming, and may be nigh at hand.

We would not attribute to Satan what belongs alone to man; but we are clear in our own convictions that no man ever did calmly and deliberately introduce a false mode of interpreting the Word of God, by which its blessed truths were obscured, its meaning mystified, and its encouragements and warnings hidden from men, without being assisted by Satanic wisdom, and Satanic craft. God, by His sovereign grace, has kept the fountain of His own Word pure, and the Bible stands forth to-day, a miracle of God's wonderful power and goodness in its preservation. The Masorites may make a commentary on the Hebrew text in the shape of points and accents, but the text itself remains pure. It is so also in the Greek original. God has preserved it. Let us rejoice in this. Let any man, then, take the Word of the Lord, and with the best translation he can get of the original text, and with the teachings of God's spirit let him seek to know the will of God, and he will not be disappointed. He will know the truth.

The Bible most clearly reveals to us the fact that the kingdoms of this world will, ere long, become the kingdom of our Lord and of his Christ, Rev. xi: 15; that Satan will be bound for a thousand years, Rev. xx: 1-4; that angels will again visit our earth in forms visible to men, John i: 51; that this whole world will come into the possession of God's people, and will be ruled by them under the special control of our Lord himself, Dan. vii: 27; Rev. v: 10; and that the whole government of earth, as now managed by the men of this world, will pass away, and that Satan's usurped dominion on earth will forever cease. Everything in the signs of the times, and in the unfolding of the prophecies, shows us that the millennial glory of the Church, and of the world is not far distant. God will not introduce that glorious dispensation without some signal displays of His power and grace. Satan, from his knowledge of the Scriptures, and from what he sees of God's plans now maturing, plainly perceives that the day of his overthrow is nigh at hand. He has now but a short time; and hence his special effort to keep the world of sinners still under his power. He is deceiving them by his false miracles, and by his pretended revelations from God, through the professed spirits of the departed, so that when our Lord shall manifest His miraculous power and wonderful workings again on the earth, the people will be disposed to attribute His divine workings and revelations to the same source whence these present manifestations spring. Thus will Satan continue to deceive the people. They will not take the warning that God may give them, and hence will not be prepared for the glories that are to be revealed in that day.

Among the signs of the times of our Lord's near approach, these Satanic delusions are not the least important. And while they exhibit to us another of Satan's plans to ruin the souls of men, they show us also how great is this power over man. Who would have thought that, from the small beginnings, in this country, of these manifestations in New York, in 1847, they would have spread all over our land, and in less than ten years would have led two millions of the people to reject Christ and his atonement, and to believe that they can, through these mediums, hold communion with the spirits of the departed, and get from them that satisfactory information concerning the future which the Bible withholds from us. But this is not all. The Spirit of God expressly declares "that in the latter times some shall depart from the faith, giving heed to seducing spirits and teachings of demons." 1 Tim. iv : 2. They will speak lies in hypocrisy. They will forbid to marry, and encourage vices of the most revolting nature, though spoken of by winning names. And such will be the power of these Satanic delusions, that all, save the elect of God, shall be deceived by them. It really seems as if these things are all being rapidly fulfilled in our day. The people would not have Jesus to reign over them, and now he is permitting them to believe a lie, the grand lie of Satan, that Jesus is not the Saviour of sinners, and that he has made no atonement for the sins of men.

Years ago, we said, while speaking on prophetic subjects, that Satan would not surrender his hold on this world without a struggle, and that his efforts to deceive the world, and to hinder the work of the Church of Christ, would be increased more and more in proportion as we approached the millennial dispensation of the Church, when Satan shall be bound and cast out of this world. And every day's experience convinces us more and more of the truth of this statement. Indeed, the Scriptures assure us that, " as it was in the days of Noah, so shall it be also in the days of the Son of man ; or so shall the coming of the Son of man be." Luke xvii : 26 ; Matt. xxiv : 37. The idea seems to be that there will be great wickedness in the world, and a great falling away from the faith in the Church. We do not suppose that any of those who are savingly united to Christ will perish—but the Church, in its organized capacity, will greatly depart from the faith and the zeal of the apostles, so that half of the virgins will be wise, and half foolish; but all will be asleep. Matt. xxv : 1–13.

All this seems to be hastening to its accomplishment. And while the Gospel is in the act of being preached, in all the world, for a witness unto all nations, and while it is gathering out of this world a people for God's name, (Acts xv : 13–17), Satan will, of course, make corresponding efforts to oppose it. His plans of opposing the progress of the Church of Christ, in this world, may all be reduced to two, viz : 1. Corrupting the Word of God; or, in some way neutralizing its power upon the hearts of the people; and 2. Dividing and distracting the Church, so that, instead of making a united and vigorous and persevering effort to spread the Gospel, the news of salvation to the ends of the earth, her efforts are spent more than is needful, in the affairs of this life, or in contending against each other.

SPIRITUALISM NOT NEW.

I. Spiritualism then, as a system, as now understood, is nothing new. It is only old error in a new form, and adapted to the refinement and the intellectualism of the age. Let any man read the history of the Church in the first and second centuries of the Christian Era in connection with the New Testament statements, and he will find there all the errors, or the germs of them, that have been used by Satan to harass the Church of God. The devil has no new plans in opposing the cause of Christ. He has used them all before. To us they may be new. We have to fight over again the battles the apostles and the Church, in past ages, have fought. Our weapons are the same that they had: and our foe is the same, and his plans and devices are the same.

With the politician, in this land, Satan sounds the alarm of "Union of Church and State!" And hence, to save the State from being injured by the little religion that the Church can get incorporated into her laws, the effort is made to heathenize the people, by excluding from the popular education the Word of God altogether. No man, no set of men can vote to legislate the Word of the Living God out from the system of instruction that is adopted for the education of our youth, without his being under the direct influence of the devil. The man may not be conscious of the fact, any more than the mediums of the present day are, but that does not alter the case. The vote is cast to shut out God and his law from the youthful mind, that, in due time, is to control the affairs of the State, when the present voters shall be dead. "The law of the Lord is perfect, converting the soul; the testimony of the Lord is sure, making wise the simple. The statutes of the Lord are right, rejoicing the heart; the commandment of the Lord is pure, (clear) enlightening the eyes. The fear of the Lord is clean (pure), enduring for ever; the judgments of the Lord are true and righteous altogether." Ps. xix: 7-10. If this be so, then any one can readily perceive why Satan should so perseveringly oppose the introduction of God's word into the soul. Educate the mind without the truth of God, and you educate it for evil here and for woe hereafter. If the Word of the Lord by God's Spirit converts the soul, then it makes inroads upon the kingdom of Satan in this world, and hence this fierce and continued opposition. See the sad effects of this exclusion of the Word of God from the minds of the youth, as they are exhibited this day, in the faith, the lives and the hopes of eight hundred millions of the human race. Oh! see the deep, deep moral night that hangs yet over them. Science and civilization, and the arts combined, can never dispel that darkness. Nothing can do it but the Word of God, blessed by His Spirit to the enlightenment and salvation of the soul. And this Word Satan would still keep from man.

But, when he cannot keep the Word of the Lord from a free circulation, as it is in this and in all Protestant lands, then his plan is to corrupt, or pervert its meaning, so that being mixed up with error, its power upon the soul is lost, and it becomes an useless weapon in the hands of him who would do battle against Satan. In the first century, and before the apostles were dead, the Gnostics arose, who denied that the books of the Old Testament were of Divine authority. They held that marriage ought to be discouraged, and that Christ was not a Divine person.

The Nicholaitans were united to the Gnostics in their heresies, and were remarkable for their unbridled licentiousness. Their deeds were such as God hated. Rev. ii: 6.

The Cerinthians, too, denied the Divinity of Christ, among other things.

And in the second century, the doctrine of Christ's Divine nature was denied, in addition to the other errors already mentioned; and Jesus was looked upon only as a man.

So that we have there the same errors that are now embodied under the name of Spiritualism. That there are some who seem favorably inclined to this form of Satanic delusion, and who think that in reality it is, in some degree, a new revelation from God, and that they really do hold intercourse with the spirits of their departed friends, we doubt not. They are good people whom Satan is endeavoring to lead astray. And if he cannot draw them away from their faith in the Word of the Lord, he will lead them to sin, as did Saul, in consulting with familiar spirits, instead of seeking light alone from God, and from His Word.

THE WITCH OF ENDOR.

Satan made Saul believe that he did in reality talk with Samuel. But he was deceived in this thing. Being forsaken of God, and knowing not what to do, he went, in open violation of God's command, to consult with evil spirits, and to get if possible, from them, the information that God withheld from him. This history is full of instruction to all of our day; and especially does it give a lesson of warning to those who are led away by the delusions of Satan now.

The history is found at length in 1 Samuel xxviii.— Bishop Patrick, Dr. Clarke, and others, hold that the spirit of Samuel did really appear, and that this was done, not through the power or magical arts of the woman, but contrary to her expectation, by the permission of God. But there is no necessity for supposing that the spirit of Samuel did actually appear. If Satan can transform himself into the appearance of an angel of light, so can he assume the appearance of any of the saints of the Lord. That Satan does, at will, assume different forms for the purpose of deception, is apparent from the Bible. These apparitions are not confined to one age or place. They occur whenever it suits Satan's purposes to take a shape or form that will aid him in his plans of deceit. It seems improbable, for the following reasons, that the spirit of Samuel did really appear. Because,

1. God refused to answer Saul by prophets, or by Urim, or by dreams, when he personally enquired of him. 1 Sam. xxviii: 6. Why then should he send Samuel from the spirit world, at the wish or conjurations of a witch, to do what he had just before refused to do?

2. Saul paid the spectre religious worship. He bowed his face to the ground and worshiped him. (Heb. *vayishtahoo.* Vulg. *adoravit.*) This adoration Samuel neither could nor would receive, Rev. xxii: 8, 9; but Satan himself could and did.

3. He pretends to have been disquieted by Saul and the witch's power. This is putting the saints of the Lord, after their departure from this world, in the power of mortals on the earth.

4. She represents the spirit of Samuel as coming up out of the ground. This accords exactly with Is. xxix: 4, which informs us that familiar spirits thus appear, and their voices issue from the ground. "And thou shalt be brought down and shalt speak out of the ground, and thy speech shall be low out of the dust, and thy voice shall be as of one that hath a familiar spirit, out of the ground, and thy speech shall whisper out of the dust."

5. The spirit of the Lord had left Saul, and an evil spirit had taken hold of him, and doubtless was still with him, and now appeared to him, dressed up like Samuel when on the earth.—1 Sam. xvi: 14.

6. The prediction of Saul's death was true as to the *fact*, but not as to the *time;* for it was not the next day that Saul died. But if the Hebrew word *machar*, rendered " to-morrow," means merely future time, then this is only what Satan might judge would be the case.

7. Saul was cut off from life for two things. The first was for disobeying God in the matter of Amelek, v. 18.— The second was for asking counsel from one who had a familiar spirit, (1. Chron. x : 13.) It appears impossible, then, that Samuel should be sent by the Lord, at the request of a witch, and thus sanction a wickedness for which Saul was killed.

8. The prediction that Saul and his sons should die on to-morrow, or soon, was true only in part. Three of Saul's sons were slain, (xxxi : 2,) but his two other sons, Armoni and Mephibosheth, lived, and were long after hanged by the Gibeonites, 2 Sam. xxi : 9, if we get the correct idea from this history.

Not to multiply reasons which might be offered, we conclude that Satan himself appeared in this case, and not one of his angels, as on ordinary occasions. And this would be sufficient to terrify the woman herself, and to account for all that had happened.

II. Satan's other plan is to distract the Church, or to divide her into fragments, and, if possible, array each separate family of the household of faith against the others.— The different denominations of Christians now on the face of the earth, are a proof of Satan's power. While we hold the great doctrines of the Gospel, yet his influence is such as to make God's people contend more earnestly for a form of faith than for the faith itself, and to spend more time and effort in defending a rite in the Church than would be needful to save many from the power of Satan. And even in the matter of Spiritualism as now developed, we doubt not but he will lead many in the Church to hand over their brethren bodily into the hands of Satan, rather than to make prayerful and faithful efforts to save them from the fowler's snare. That Spiritualism, as it is now developed in our midst, is a device of Satan to oppose, in anticipation, the coming and kingdom of our Lord, we cannot doubt. Our efforts should be, in love, to save, not destroy; to compassionate, not condemn those who may be possessed by Satan. And if the Church of Christ, at first, had the power to cast out demons, why may she not do so yet? Some kinds of demons can be dispossessed only by prayer and fasting. If God's people would seek from Him the faith they need, they may not only keep themselves out of the power of these evil spirits, but may cast them out of those who are now possessed. So saith our Lord; and so we believe.—Mark xvi: 17, 18.

CONCLUSION.

Not to extend these remarks any farther, we would say to any who have not thought it labor lost to read these pages, to put no confidence in the revelations that may be made by Satan and his angels through those whom he has employed as mediums. If they should at any time accord with the truth, that is only designed by him to win the confidence of the deceived, so that Satan may the more easily deceive them to their final undoing. The awful language of the apostle Paul, in 2 Thess. ii: 11, 12, is not without its solemn significancy at the present time,— " For this cause God shall send them strong delusion, that they should believe a lie; that they all might be damned who believe not the truth, but had pleasure in unrighteousness."

"Resist the Devil and he will flee from you," is both the command and the promise of the Lord. "Have no fellowship with these unfruitful works of darkness, but rather reprove them. Put on the whole armor of God, that ye may be able to stand against the wiles of the devil; for we wrestle not against flesh and blood, but against principalities and powers; against the rulers of the darkness of this world; against wicked spirits in the heavenly places, *en tois epouraniois.*"—Eph. vi: 11, 12.

We quote, as very appropriate, at the close of these remarks, the language of one who had been a warm advocate of Spiritualism, and who wrote and published much in its favor, but who, having seen the delusion in its right light, sends forth his warning voice to those who are yet led captive by Satan unto his will. He says:

"Now, after a long and constant watchfulness, seeing for months and years its progress and its practical workings upon its devotees, its believers, and its mediums, we are compelled to speak our honest conviction, which is, that the manifestations coming through the acknowledged mediums, who are designated as rapping, tipping, writing, and entranced mediums, have a baneful influence upon believers, and create discord and confusion; that the generality of these teachings inculcate false ideas, approve of selfish, individual acts, and endorse theories and principles which, when carried out, *debase* and make men *little better than the brute.* These are among the fruits of modern Spiritualism, and we do not hesitate to say that we believe if these manifestations are continued to be received, and to be as little understood as they are, and have been since they made their appearance at Rochester, and mortals are to be deceived by their false, fascinating, and snake-like charming powers which go with them, the day will come when the world will require the appearance of another Saviour [not another, but the Saviour himself] to redeem the world from its departing from Christ's warnings."

Again he adds—" Seeing, as we have, the gradual progress it makes with its believers, particularly its mediums, from lives of *morality* to those of *sensuality* and *immorality*, gradually, and cautiously undermining the foundation of good principles, we look back with amazement to the radical change which a few months will bring about in individuals, for its tendency is to approve and endorse each individual act and character, however good or bad these acts may be."

He concludes by saying—" We desire to send forth our warning voice, and if our humble position, as the head of a public journal, our known advocacy of Spiritualism, our experience, and the conspicuous part we have played among its believers, the honesty and the fearlessness with which we have defended the subject, will weigh anything in our favor, we desire that our opinions may be received, and those who are moving passively down the rushing rapids to destruction, should pause, ere it be too late, and save themselves from the blasting influence which those manifestations are causing."—*J. F. Whitney, Ed. N. Y. Pathfinder.*

Here is a warning voice from a gentleman of whom we have no knowledge further than what we obtain from these brief extracts from his paper. But it is a warning most seasonable, kind, and true. May it be fully heeded. And may God give grace to those who are now deceived by the adversary, so that they may acknowledge the truth as it is in Christ Jesus, and that they may recover themselves out of the snare of the devil. 2 Tim. ii : 26.

To all we would say—identify yourselves with the cause of Christ—love him and his cause sincerely.—Serve him faithfully. Rely for salvation on his atonement alone.— Walk by faith, and lead a holy life, and in the end you will triumph over Satan and all your spiritual foes. Then will you be able to sing the victor's song of "Glory to God and to the Lamb:" and to shout aloud with a grateful heart, "thanks be to God who giveth us the victory through our Lord Jesus Christ." And in the language of the apostle we would say—"Yet I would have you wise unto that which is good, and simple (*akeraious*, blameless) in that which is evil. And the God of peace shall bruise Satan under your feet shortly. The grace of our Lord Jesus Christ be with you. Amen." Rom. xvi : 19-20.

www.ingramcontent.com/pod-product-compliance
Lightning Source LLC
Chambersburg PA
CBHW021942160426
43195CB00011B/1194